1
3
Pappenheim, Fritz.
    The alienation of modern man; an
interpretation based on Marx and
Tonnies. New York, Monthly Review
Press, 1959.
    189 p. 22 cm.

THE ALIENATION OF MODERN MAN

An Interpretation Based
On Marx and Tönnies

A caza de dientes.

The Alienation
of Modern Man

*AN INTERPRETATION BASED
ON MARX AND TÖNNIES*

Fritz Pappenheim

 Modern Reader Paperbacks
New York and London

301, 15
PAPPEN

TO YVONNE

CONTENTS

THE ALIENATION OF MODERN MAN

An Interpretation Based
on Marx and Tönnies

INTRODUCTION

AMONG GOYA'S "CAPRICHOS" is one which the artist called "A caza de dientes" (On the Hunt for Teeth.) The etching shows a woman who, possessed by the superstition that the teeth of a hanged man can yield magic power, has sneaked up to a body dangling from a noose. Holding a piece of cloth between the corpse and her averted face, she is torn between horror and a determination to get hold of the invaluable teeth. Standing on tiptoe, her arm stretched out, with a shudder of revulsion she makes her hand reach the mouth of the stiff, dead body.

The morbidity of an age which has long gone by? We should not be too sure of such an interpretation. There is much evidence that Goya's etching has not lost its significance in the world of today. Some years ago a popular magazine published the results of a photographic contest. An award was made for the picture which gave the freshest on-the-spot news. One of the photos chosen presented a traffic accident in which two automobiles were completely demolished, and showed the pain-stricken face of one of the victims in the moment before death.

The motives of the woman in Goya's etching and of the photographer who participated successfully in the prize contest may have been quite different. The one was driven by superstition; the second by the desire for monetary gain or recognition. There seems however to be an

11

affinity between the two individuals. Both of them are so absorbed in the relentless pursuit of their interests that this pursuit shapes every phase of their encounter with reality. Nothing they experience has a meaning in itself; nothing counts for them unless it can be turned into a means for attaining their ends. Even death is not exempt. Coming face to face with it, they are able to relate only to the one phase of it which they calculate is of advantage to them, while they remain indifferent onlookers before the other aspect, which to them is a useless remainder, the impact of death itself.

Can we say that this aloofness and lack of participation are traits characteristic only of persons like the woman in Goya's etching or like the photographer who, witnessing the pain of another human being, thinks solely of using his camera? Such a consoling thought would not be realistic. There seems to be a tendency in all of us to become indifferent bystanders. In the way we associate with other people or respond to important happenings we tend toward a fragmentary encounter. We do not relate to the other person as a whole or to the event as a whole, but we isolate the one part which is important to us and remain more or less remote observers of the rest.

The person who thus splits the real into two parts becomes divided in his own self. So deep is the cleavage which goes through the woman in Goya's etching that the artist seems to show her as two human beings who are insulated from each other, the one moving toward a coveted prize, the other miserably looking away from her own action. There is something uncanny in the condition of man when he has become a stranger to himself; but it is a fate which shapes the lives of many of us. We seem to be caught in a frightening contradiction. In order to assert ourselves as individuals, we relate only to those phases of reality which seem to promote the attainment of our objectives and we remain divorced from the rest of it. But the further we drive this separation, the deeper grows the rift within ourselves.

The "company wife" who, concerned about her husband's career, chooses her friends more among the "right people" than among those to whom she feels drawn; the individuals who, for reasons of social prestige or in consideration of professional or business interests, join the church which gives a relatively high degree of respectability rather than the one which represents their religious backgrounds and beliefs; the political leader who, realizing that his struggle for an unpopular cause might doom his chances for re-election, abandons his convictions to secure his political future; the painter who, committed to creative but not generally accepted ideas, gives up the struggle of the lonely artist and accepts the attractive fees and the security of a job in an advertising agency—all these persons show how those who are estranged from what is real can no longer be themselves.

The individual's alienation from everything which has no bearing on the pursuit of his interests does not necessarily enter into his consciousness; nor does he always become aware of the estrangement from his own self or feel it as a disquieting experience. As a result of his detachment, the alienated man is often able to achieve great successes. These, as long as they continue, engender a certain numbness, which makes it hard for him to realize his own estrangement. Only in times of crisis does he start to sense it.

Societies too are often unperturbed by trends toward alienation, a fact which is illustrated by the history of the word "alienation." In its philosophical sense the term was first used by Fichte and Hegel at the beginning of the nineteenth century, though at that time its influence was confined to small groups of their disciples. It was incorporated into sociological theory in the forties of that century, when Marx centered his interpretation of the capitalist era upon the concept of self-alienation. But the concept did not exercise this influence for any length of time, and it became almost forgotten in the period which followed. Now, approximately one hundred years later, it has come again to the foreground and has become almost a catchword, even in circles which have little sympathy with Marxian thought. This may well be due to the years of continuing crisis which have forced on our awareness the problem of human estrangement.

Today, concern about man's alienation is expressed by many: by theologians and philosophers who warn that advances in scientific knowledge do not enable us to penetrate the mystery of Being, and do not bridge but often widen the gulf between the knower and the reality he tries to understand; by psychiatrists who try to help their patients return from the world of illusion to reality; by critics of the increasing mechanization of life who challenge the optimistic expectation that technological progress will automatically lead to the enrichment of human lives; by political scientists who note that even democratic institutions have failed to bring about genuine participation by the masses in the great issues of our period.

Some of these views, described more fully in the first chapters of this book, go back to ideas which were developed fifty years ago by the sociologist and philosopher Georg Simmel and which were later articulated by spokesmen for existential philosophy, by the Roman Catholic scholar Romano Guardini, and by others. These authors have contributed much to the understanding of significant examples of human estrangement. However they have been tempted to focus on *specific* forms of alienation without seeing how they are interrelated, without asking whether these seemingly isolated manifestations do not form part of a predominant contemporary trend. As long as we fail to ask this question we shall not arrive at a real understanding of the problem. Facing the situations of pain and conflict to which the alienated man is exposed, we shall see our sufferings as due to unfortunate mishaps. Instead of coming to grips with the inherent forces of alienation we shall merely react with feelings of nostalgia and sadness, or with complaints and empty protests.

This book tries to avoid such a mistake. Wilhelm Dilthey has said that the manifestations of the energy which shapes an era are akin to one another. This insight applies to the understanding of alienation. The preoccupation with single forms of alienation should not obscure the awareness of links between them. We should not dismiss in advance the question as to whether these seemingly isolated expressions do not spring from the same source, from the basic direction of our period and its social structure.

But do we not oversimplify the problem when we relate alienation to a specific period of history instead of seeing it as rooted in the human condition? Many readers will raise this question here and will reiterate it as they go on to other parts of the book. This seems to the author a serious challenge, and he attempts to answer it at length in the last chapters. Here it is only possible to warn of a misunderstanding that could arise. The thesis that the forces of alienation *predominate* in our era does not imply that they did not exist in previous ages. It does assert that they have gained greatly in intensity and significance in the modern world. To relate this development to the social structure of our period is the aim of this book.

In pursuing this task we go back to some of Marx's earlier writings and especially to the *Oekonomisch-Philosophische Manuskripte* (1844) which, although much discussed at present in France, Germany, and England, has remained almost unknown in this country. It is one of our aims to direct the American reader's attention to the importance of these manuscripts, only parts of which have so far been translated into English. For this reason we have quoted extensively from them, especially in Chapter Four. (A complete English translation has been announced by the British publishers Lawrence & Wishart.)

The controversy about Marx's work is still, perhaps now more than ever, dominated by dogmatic defense on the one side and by passionate rejection on the other side. Thus it may be sheer boldness to expect any of the statements we have selected from the *Manuscripts* to be examined in a calm and unprejudiced fashion. Yet the most loyal follower cannot afford to ignore ideas of Marx because they do not fit in with views generally attributed to him. And the most determined opponent must realize that a tendency to underestimate the true position and strength of the enemy has usually led to mistakes for which a high price had to be paid.

We dwell also on the writings of Ferdinand Tönnies (1855-1936), because in our view they have contributed much to the understanding of the relationship between man's alienation and society. Although this German scholar's name appeared as early as 1906 among the advisory editors of the *American Journal of Sociology*, his work *Gemeinschaft und Gesellschaft*, which has been quoted in many a sociological text and paper, has not really been assimilated and has remained relatively unknown. The widely held interpretation that it was written out of a nostalgic desire to return to the past has kept many sociologists from recognizing its lasting significance. Yet we believe that Tönnies' work has great relevance today. Its basic concepts, which make it possible to analyze social structures without isolating them from the historical reality in which they are imbedded, give important insights into the direction in which modern society is moving.

The author acknowledges that this essay is not written in a spirit of detached neutrality but originates from a premise. He believes that a society dominated by the forces of alienation stifles the fulfilment of human potentialities, that in such a society respect for the individual and for the dignity of man cannot be implemented but will remain in the realm of ideas and philosophic pronouncements. Whether the value judgment which motivates this book deprives it of objectivity is for the reader to decide.

CHAPTER ONE

The Mood of Our Age: Awareness
of Man's Alienation

RESTORING CITIES and bridges, technological equipment and
economic-financial institutions, seems to go faster than
rebuilding the spirit of a world which has undergone the
destruction of modern war. This appears to be a point of
agreement in many otherwise varying reports which have
come to us from Europe after World War II. In spite of
the amazing speed with which the physical reconstruction
has been carried out, it seems that gloom and despair still
retain a strong grip on European thinking.

It would be an oversimplification to attribute this turn
towards pessimism only to the aftermath of the last war
and to the fear of a new one. It should not be overlooked
that the part of the world known as Western civilization
has been suffering for a long time from an inner crisis.
The present leaning towards nihilism is nothing but a
new expression of the mood of doubt that followed the
prevalence of belief—belief in the greatness of man, the
infiniteness of progress, and the sovereignty of reason—
characteristic of the eighteenth and nineteenth centuries.

This feeling of despair not only speaks to us from Spengler's writings but also dominates the thinking of authors whose contributions are very much above the writings of this sensational prophet of doom. Georg Simmel, who has considerably influenced contemporary philosophy and sociology both in Europe and in the United States, has expressed in his works the mood of skepticism which arose in the first decades of this century.[1] His essay "Der Konflikt der Modernen Kultur" reflects the growing fear—in our day reiterated by the existentialists—that man cannot be himself, that he is destined to remain a stranger in the world in which he lives.

According to Simmel, an inner conflict, stemming from the antagonism between life and form, can be seen in the development of most civilizations. The creative movement of life in a civilization tends to express itself in law, technology, art, science, and religion. Although the purpose of these expressions is to implement and to protect the life which engendered them, they reveal an immanent tendency to follow a direction and a rhythm of their own, independent of and divorced from the energies of life which brought them into being. At the moment of their emergence they might correspond to the life which created them; but as they unfold they appear to fall into stubborn disconnection, even into a state of opposition. They are bound to become rigid, to stand by themselves, and to take on a measure of imperviousness. Thus they tend to acquire continuity, even a timeless character: in a word, they become *forms*.

Without these forms the creative life could not have become manifest. It continuously produces them. Yet it

20

keeps on flowing like a ceaseless stream, forever engendering new forms but immediately opposing them in their solidity and permanence. Thus, rapidly or slowly, the energies of life gnaw at every cultural formation, once it has emerged. As one formation evolves its successor develops beneath it and eventually, after a short or a lengthy struggle, replaces it.

This perennial opposition between life and form—Simmel believes for reasons which he does not analyze—is intensified and enhanced in our age. He thinks that life now is no longer in revolt against these or those specific forms which it finds alien and imposed, but against forms as such, against the principle of form. Therefore he feels that the moralists who praise the olden times with their emphasis on style and form are not so wrong when they complain about the "formlessness" or informality predominating in the present period. But they overlook the fact that what is happening is not just something negative, the dying of traditional form: the energy that rejects these forms is an entirely positive impulse for life.

Writing in a period which witnessed the great response to Bergson's ideas, Simmel does not find it hard to prove his thesis that the cult of life has deeply influenced the philosophical outlook of our age. He sees every period in history as producing one specific idea which, in spite of many variations, disguises, and oppositions, dominates that era as its secret king. In classical Greece this central concept was the idea of being; in the Middle Ages, the idea of God; in the Renaissance, the idea of nature; in the seventeenth century, the idea of natural law. During the eighteenth century the individual becomes the central theme; and in the twentieth century the concept of life excels all others in its appeal to us and its influence upon our outlook.

With extraordinary sensitivity, Simmel analyzes the most important cultural trends of the period from the end of the nineteenth century to the time of World War I and shows how deeply the idea of life pulses in them.

In the realm of art he describes how the tendency of the Expressionist painters to break away from specific and objective content reflects the struggle of life to be its own authentic self. The life emanating from the artist's inner self should follow its own inherent law, an objective which would be entirely unattainable if the artist aimed at creating a likeness to a form in the outside world.

Simmel believes that he can recognize a similar trend in the prevailing philosophical thinking of his period. He shows how the pragmatists' revolt against tradition, their insistence that no abstract and timeless system of reason but only the forces of life can provide us with the criteria for truth, is kindred to the thesis developed by Bergson and his school that the essence of being is life and that therefore it can only be seized from within, by the forces of intuitive understanding rather than by means of intellectual analysis.

In the realm of religion Simmel notices a trend to divorce the religious experience, not only from traditional forms and cults, but also from the encounter with the dimension of transcendence. In an early work he points out that for many of his contemporaries religion has become an attitude towards life, that the attachment of the devoted child to his parents, of the elated patriot to his country, of the enthusiastic cosmopolitan to the cause of humanity, of the workman to his class, of the nobleman to his caste, has a religious quality.[2] This way of looking at religion may already have been intimated by some mystics of the past. Simmel believes it inspired Angelus Silesius' words:

> Der Heil'ge, wenn er trinkt,
> Gefallet Gott so wohl
> Wie wenn er bet' und singt.

> When the saint drinks
> He pleases God as much
> As when he prays and sings.

But in spite of this early anticipation, the tendency to detach religion, not only from revered forms of worship, but also from revelations of the absolute and the divine is a specific manifestation of the mind of contemporary man.

To show that the conflict between form and life has reached even the most personal and intimate aspects of human relations, Simmel describes the development of attitudes toward sex under the impact of modern civilization. He describes the opposition to prevailing conditions, and particularly the criticism advanced by a movement called New Ethics whose ideas were proclaimed by few but shared by many. This criticism was directed particularly against two institutions of decisive importance for the predominating pattern of sexual relations—modern marriage and prostitution. Both have the tendency to

direct sex life into channels which destroy its true meaning and degrade it, instead of protecting and enhancing
it. Marriage, often "contracted" out of conventional or
utilitarian considerations or for the sake of conforming
to traditional patterns and often maintained only in view
of rigid and inflexible legal rules which are completely
remote from the needs of modern man, tends to result in
cruelty and to become a form which depersonalizes and
degrades the genuine love impulse. It shares this effect
with prostitution, which as a consequence of many taboos
observed by our society has become a dominating and
all-but-legal institution. Prostitution likewise presses the
sexual life of the individual into forms which allow only
a completely impersonal relationship and represent the
deepest negation of a genuine love bond.

All the examples which Simmel presents reflect contemporary man's fear that his individuality will be destroyed, that he is living under conditions which compel
him to become estranged from his own self. There are
numerous indications that this apprehension is one of
the decisive forces in the thinking of modern man. It
accounts in our opinion for the strong appeal of existential
philosophy. We may criticize this movement as obscure,
as abandoning the ways of reason and yielding to impulse
and to undisciplined emotionalism. But we should not
ignore the fact that many persons are fascinated by the
existentialists' demand that the individual should become
that which he is, even if this commitment to his own self,
to his "authentic existence," means that he has to accept
the fate of the lonely "outsider."

Existential philosophy is essentially a revolt against

the belief, deeply rooted in the development of modern thought, that truth can be ascertained only through detachment, that the cognitive act requires a radical separation between the knower, represented as the subject, and the reality to be known, represented as the object. There is no question that this idea has greatly advanced our knowledge, especially in the realm of natural sciences. Without it the development of our most essential scientific methods would not have been achieved. Yet there has been a considerable protest against the tendency to isolate man's cognitive function from the rest of his being and to destroy his unity and his universality by divesting him of all but his intellectual qualities, thus reducing him to a mere epistemological subject. There has likewise been a deep concern about the other aspect of the detached approach which turns the world with all its fullness and its rich coloring into a mere object of scientific inquiry.

Already in the nineteenth century there could be heard the voices of a few lonely thinkers who recognized the danger lying in the split between subject and object. Kierkegaard expressed his disdain for the merely "cognitive subject," whom he confronted with the existential thinker. He argued that "knowledge has a relationship to the knower, who is essentially an existing individual, and that for this reason all essential knowledge is essentially related to existence." A thinker as different from Kierkegaard as Feuerbach insisted: "Do not wish to be a philosopher in contrast to being a man . . . do not think as a thinker . . . think as a living, real being . . . think in Existence."[3]

But these ideas reflecting concern over the split between subject and object, though they were expressed in similar terms by Nietzsche and by Marx before him, did not have much impact on the thinking of the nineteenth century. The situation changed during the first decades of this century, when a larger group of individuals became disturbed by an awareness that the vast progress of knowledge had left the gulf between the knowing subject and the reality he faces unbridged. Therefore they responded strongly when the philosopher Edmund Husserl, founder of the phenomenological school of thought, tried to cope with the difficulties in overcoming the knower's remoteness from the known. He described as a great error the belief that philosophy or science had succeeded in eliminating this distance. His teaching was presented in difficult and abstract language and was readily accessible only to a small group of colleagues and disciples. But it became a gripping message for an age that had grown aware of the separation between subject and object and saw a new hope in his plea for "a return to the objects themselves."

In seeking this objective Husserl differentiates, like the medieval scholastics, between *existentia* and *essentia*. He is concerned with essences and our knowledge of them. It is true, Husserl says, that we cannot reach them by means of sensory perception. But he suggests that we liberate ourselves from the positivistic prejudice which recognizes only those experiences as valid that have been acquired by sensory perception. If we overcome this narrowness, Husserl believes, we shall realize that essences can be made experienceable, that they can be grasped and "seen" intuitively. This envisagement of essences has nothing to do with a sudden revelation and is not an easy task. It can only be achieved by a long and often difficult preparation, an arduous method which Husserl calls phenomenological reduction. This procedure has various phases which we cannot describe in detail. We can say, however, that the objective of phenomenological reduction is to suspend all consideration of the existing world, to put the factual into brackets. This can be achieved, Husserl believes, because man's mind has the power to differentiate between *existentia* and *essentia,* to set aside existences, and to attain pure consciousness of essences.

This basic thought of the phenomenological school has a strong affinity with certain trends in contemporary art, as Ludwig Binswanger has shown. To illustrate the relationship Binswanger selects Franz Marc's painting *The Blue Horses.* In this painting the artist, as he indicates by the choice of color, is utterly unconcerned about horses as they actually exist. But by this very approach his painting conveys to us the essence of horse, one could say "horsiness," very much more strongly than many paintings which aim at a representation of nature as it exists.[4]

It was hoped that in the intuitive grasping of essences a way had been found to bridge the gulf between subject and object. Many intellectuals, who had known the despair of an age in which this split left the individual with nothing but crumbling certainties, turned to Husserl's program with deep and ardent expectation. But soon it was felt that his answer was unsatisfactory, that it did not help to bridge the chasm between man's mind and the outside world. Many of his once enthusiastic followers turned away from him. They revolted against Husserl's attempt to put man and his world into brackets in order to reach impersonal and timeless consciousness. The cognitive act, they insisted, is not based on neutrality but on deepest participation. By separating truth from human existence, by accepting the detached form of knowing as the only road toward truth, Husserl, they argued, had not overcome, but had deepened, the estrangement between man's mind and the outside world.

These existential philosophers opposed Husserl's separation of essence and existence, his claim that we can grasp the essence of objects regardless of whether they actually exist. They saw a great danger in the view that essences are, so to speak, neutral toward their forms of realization and are detachable from them. They emphasized that the concept of essence is a static one and can be applied only to those forms of reality which are characterized by a fixed and unchangeable nature. Therefore it is completely inadequate for the understanding of the human person. All attempts to describe man by explaining his essence will result in reducing him to a thing, as evidenced by Descartes' definition of man as *res cogitans*, a thing that thinks. Such an approach overlooks the fact that man differs from an object in that he is not predetermined by properties but creates himself through his own choices and acts. Far from being the product of his qualities, he is what he spontaneously decides to be. He improvises and is fundamentally unpredictable. Now he is a dedicated and courageous fighter for a common cause; a short while later, he is a cowardly traitor. Today he is a brutal bully; tomorrow a gentle, helpful friend.

Though the leading exponents of existential philosophy differ in many of their ideas, they all stress the view that the human self does not coincide with the individual's basic properties. It is capable of breaking away from and transcending its own properties, and even external conditions of its environment. In his moving essay "La République du Silence," Sartre has written a few sentences which not only describe the attitude of his countrymen during the Nazi occupation but convey at the same time the indeterministic orientation of existentialist thought:

We were never more free than during the German occupation. We had lost all our rights, beginning with the right to talk. Every day we were insulted to our faces and had to take it in silence. Under one pretext or another, as workers, Jews, or political prisoners, we were deported EN MASSE. Everywhere, on billboards, in the newspapers, on the screen, we encountered the revolting and insipid picture of ourselves that our oppressors wanted us to accept. And, because of all this, we were free. Because the Nazi venom seeped even into our thoughts, every accurate thought was a conquest. Because an all-powerful police tried to force us to hold our tongues, every word took on the value of a declaration of principles. Because we were hunted down, every one of our gestures had the weight of a solemn commitment. . . . And the choice that each of us made of his life and of his being was an authentic choice because it was made face to face with death, because it could always have been expressed in these terms: "Rather death than. . . ." And here I am not speaking of the elite among us who were real Resistants, but of all Frenchmen who, at every hour of the night and day throughout

29

four years, answered NO. . . . Thus the basic question of liberty itself was posed, and we were brought to the verge of the deepest knowledge that man can have of himself. For the secret of a man is not his Oedipus complex or his inferiority complex: it is the limit of his own liberty, his capacity for resisting torture and death.[5]

Ortega y Gasset, who is in many ways a precursor of existentialist thought, has stated that the static meaning of the term "to be" makes it entirely inadequate to describe man's existence. We cannot say, he insists, that man "is" but only that he is on the way to be this or that.[6] This formulation expresses well the meaning of the existentialists' view that the core of man's existence is possibility. For them existence is being which in every moment transcends itself, which, since it is directed toward the future, is constantly in advance of itself. Thus they consider man's existence as his concern to become what he is and to be what he has to become. Heidegger and also the French existentialists proclaim the paradox that man, in order to exist, has to throw himself toward his own being. Therefore they call his existence a pro-ject, emphasizing the original meaning of this term as derived from the Latin word *jacere* (to cast, throw). They add that project in this sense has nothing to do with a conscious or rationally designed plan: instead it indicates that man's existence has to move beyond itself in order to move toward itself.

Will man follow this course? If existence is nothing but possibility, man's destiny is a hard one. At every moment he faces various alternatives between which he has to choose. This constitutes his freedom, but it thrusts upon him a frightening burden of responsibility. He is forced into cruel situations, in which a decision for any of the various possibilities will be portentous and will reveal the close relationship between freedom and guilt. Thus man does not cherish his sovereignty, which not only enables but *compels* him to make his own choices. He feels himself condemned to be free (Sartre). He tries to avoid a state of being in which he must ceaselessly decide for himself. But when man seeks to evade the decisions with which he is faced, he is really attempting to escape from his own self. He tries to escape what he cannot escape . . . what he is.[7] Yet so deep is his anguish that he feels himself driven to slip away into a world in which he is not any longer committed to his own self but can follow the choices of "the others," of that anonymous collective which is called "they." This is a totally depersonalized way of being, so general and inarticulate that Heidegger characterizes it by using the German pronoun *man*, a most impersonal and neutral term, meaning "one of many." It is well fitted to reveal the innermost nature of a world where everyone is "the other one" and nobody is his own self, and where the meaning of the personal pronoun has been lost to such an extent that statements like "I think," "I prefer," "I act" have become empty forms.

Heidegger tells us that if man tends to flee from himself and to plunge from the height of solitude into the public lowlands of the many we should not see in this fall a descent into inquietude and crisis. Quite the contrary: to exist simply as one of the many "exercises a profoundly appeasing influence as if everything was in the best order."[8] Tempting as this appeasement is, man cannot obtain it without paying a high price. He must cease to be himself, he must become estranged from his own self.

Simmel described the triumph of form over life, the danger that man's surrender to form might make it increasingly difficult for him to be his own self. Unlike the existentialists, he struggled to hold on to his faith in human achievement and to keep it from being destroyed by a mood of doubt and despair. He did not view the conflict between form and life simply as a threat or crisis, but saw it as the indispensable basis for the birth of new forms better adapted to the emerging forces of life. This illustrates his tendency to recognize the stumbling blocks to the development of mankind but to emphasize their meaning as challenges.[9] Heidegger and most of the existential philosophers offer us a more gloomy picture of human existence. Man is alienated from reality, as the result of a split between subject and object which detached knowledge does not heal but deepens. He is estranged from himself, because in flight from himself he lets his existence be plunged down into the inauthenticity of the anonymous crowd. The transition from Simmel's ideas to those of the existentialists is not merely a development in the realm of philosophical thought. It reflects a deep change in the general character of the times—from conditions in the first decades of this century, when in spite of some forebodings the belief in progress was still prevalent, to the thirties and after, when tragic events engendered the disillusionment and despair expressed in existentialist pessimism.

In describing man as a stranger in the world, existential philosophy has formulated one of the central experiences of our age. Heidegger once wrote: "Homelessness is becoming a world fate." The same metaphor is used to symbolize modern man's deepest fear by the poets and novelists who have best understood the inquietude of our time.

Who has no home now will not build one any more.
Who is alone now will remain alone[10]

writes Rilke. In one of his later poems he compares man to a stranger who from his window looks out into the dark, abandoned street of an unfamiliar and inhospitable town:

The new city was still to me as though denied and the unresponsive landscape spread its darkness as though I were not there. The nearest things did not bother to reveal themselves to me. The alley climbed to the street light. I saw how alien it was. Across the way a room was warmly lighted by a lamp. It made me feel included. They sensed this and drew the shutters.[11]

The nostalgia of man suffering from the loneliness and pain of an anonymous existence is expressed in Phyllis McGinley's "Midcentury Love Letter":

Stay near me. Speak my name. Oh do not wander
By a thought's span, heart's impulse, from the light
We kindle here. You are my sole defender
(As I am yours) in this precipitous night,
Which over earth, till common landmarks alter,

33

Is falling, without stars, and bitter cold . . . .
Stay near me. Spirit, perishable as bone,
In no such winter can survive alone.[12]

Man's alienation and his anonymous way of existing
have been described with methodic and terrifying pre
cision by Kafka, who wrote of himself: "I am separated
from all things by a hollow space, and I do not even reach
to its boundaries."[13] The main characters in the novels
The Trial and *The Castle* are completely depersonalized
and reduced to mere masks. This loss of identity leads to a
state of radical anonymity, which the author symbolizes
by not using a name but merely a letter of the alphabet
to refer to them.

American novelists also have described man's fate of
alienation and homelessness. We shall mention only
Thomas Wolfe, who devotes much of his work to record-
ing the painful experience of the uprooted man, the nostalgic exile and wanderer. Wolfe sums it up in the symbolic
words of Eugene Gant, the central figure of "The Return
of the Prodigal": "What did you come home for? . . .
You know now that you can't go home again!"[14]

Many individuals have found their own lives portrayed
in Arthur Miller's *Death of a Salesman*. It shows Willy
Loman—the "other-directed man" personified—striving
all his life to be popular and "liked" but remaining abso-
lutely lonesome and irrelevant, forever dreaming that
"personality always wins the day" but in reality destined,
as his wife fears, "to fall into his grave like an old dog."
His motto is: Start big and you'll end big. He advises his
son: "Get right down the field under the ball, and when

you hit, hit low and hit hard." He does not realize that he himself is kicked around and that his whole existence is summed up in the word with which one of the women in the play describes her life: "a football."[15]

The strong response to the writers from whom we have quoted reflects in our view a growing contemporary concern about man's isolation and alienation. This does not mean, however, that all those who are concerned visualize this estrangement in the same way that the existentialists do. Unlike those followers of Heidegger and Sartre who look on man's alienation and homelessness as his eternal fate, many of those who turn to the writers we have mentioned attribute the alienation to historical events. They refer, for example, to the two world wars in this century; to the rise of totalitarian governments, with their disregard for the sacredness of the human person; to gas chambers and all the brutalities to which victims of the concentration camps and of brain washing have been subjected. They sometimes mention the abrupt economic changes which have accompanied the international conflicts and which have intensified the insecurity and strain in the living conditions of millions of people.

This explanation, although right in emphasizing the historical aspect of man's alienation, must be challenged, because it is based on a widely held but questionable assumption. It attributes the rise of alienation to a few isolated and almost fortuitous occurrences which have broken in upon the lives of the present generation—so to speak—from the outside. Such a premise is of dubious merit because it tends unduly to limit the scope of inquiry. It leads us to ignore from the outset significant developments which—as the following pages will try to bring out—show that alienation is manifest in all realms of modern life, that its existence is not just the result of certain accidents of recent history but exemplifies one of the basic trends of our age.

CHAPTER TWO

Technology and Alienation

"THE MODERN AGE in its essential aspects is drawing to a close," says Romano Guardini at the beginning of his book *Die Macht* (Power).[1] This statement formulates a growing awareness which is expressed by numerous contemporary authors. Many of them refer to our changing attitude toward the machine. They emphasize that the belief in the blessings of technological advancement, which epitomizes the modern outlook, has been considerably weakened and has yielded to a clearer insight into the antagonism between the machine and the human soul.

It is true that many individuals in Europe and in this country are convinced that the machine threatens the spiritual values of mankind. They find it hard to understand the burning faith in technological progress which inspired previous generations. This faith in technology grew out of the situation man faced in the centuries after the decline of the medieval world. The individual, who until then had considered himself integrated into a universal order embracing his physical and spiritual existence, found himself uprooted and banished from the supernatural dwellings which had sheltered him in the days of his unshaken religious certainty. Now he was driven to build himself a new home, the foundation of which had to be in the life of this world.[2] To make this earthly abode safer and friendlier became an imperative challenge. Man could respond to the extent to which he succeeded in understanding and mastering the forces of nature and utilizing them for his own purposes. Thus the ground was prepared for man's appeal to the machine. Its reign seemed to promise the reign of man's autonomy. Technological progress became identified with human progress.

The image of man underlying the hopeful acceptance of the machine is different from that of the Middle Ages, but it is not anti-religious. It expresses the very essence of religious thinking as it developed after the eclipse of the medieval outlook, seeking to steer a course equally distant from spiritual contemplation and materialistic worldliness. It is known that this relationship between religious ideas and the glorification of work as discipline led Max Weber and his school to a thesis which traces the rise of capitalism to the influence of Protestant ethics. Although, for reasons which cannot be stated here, this theory is unacceptable as an adequate historical explanation of the origins of modern capitalism, it is true that theological arguments have often been presented in defense of machine production as the most effective way to utilize the blessings of this earth bestowed on us by the divine creator.

This way of thinking has not been confined to the beginnings of the industrial age, but has continued into the present century. As one of many examples we select a book written a few years before the outbreak of World War I, *Ethik und Kapitalismus* by Gottfried Traub. For the author, a Protestant theologian, it is quite evident that those who are concerned with the ethics of Christianity ought to welcome every victory of technology. If we strive earnestly for a higher stage of morality, Traub argues, we must overcome patriarchal conditions and antiquated methods of production, we must adopt the most productive work instruments, the methods that promise the highest yield, and the most advanced forms of plant management. We ought never to lose sight of the close relationship between technology and a truly human way of existing. We should realize that to work for technological progress is far more than to aim at rendering our external life more comfortable: it is a way to worship God.[3]

Today we seem to have grown far away from this trust in the machine, and many of our contemporaries react with a condescending smile to the idea of progress. The change, of course, did not come over night. Even in the past when the achievements of modern technology were loudly praised, cautioning and skeptical voices made themselves heard. In those days, however, the accusations against the machine were quite different from its indictment in our present world. In the past the attacks came primarily from men who were disturbed more by the economic effects of rapid industrialization than by its impact on man's soul. There were of course some romantic writers who, repelled by the ugliness and monotony of the factory, harked back to the idyllic workshop of the craftsman or to the quiet fields where the peasant tilled the soil. However, this aesthetic nostalgia for the past carried less weight than the revolt against the machine which grew out of the plight of those whose very livelihood was threatened by changing production methods. The finest arguments to the effect that the advance of technology meant progress and contributed to man's liberation could not allay their fears. The threatened workmen continued to regard the new engines as their enemies; and their hatred sometimes exploded in violent riots, resulting in considerable destruction of machinery.[4]

The seriousness of the dangers which the workmen faced is illustrated by the seventeenth and eighteenth century decrees prohibiting use of the so-called ribbon loom, in both England and Germany. The Mayor of Danzig, according to an account written by the Abbé Lancellotti in 1579, had the inventor of a very ingenious weaving machine secretly killed.[5]

Today attacks on the idea of technological progress do not come primarily from economic circles but from groups who are concerned about spiritual and cultural values. These critics believe that there is an antithesis between technology and man's soul, a gap which cannot be bridged. As a consequence, they believe that we have become victims of a development by which technology has gained and man has lost. This pessimistic view, expressed by authors like Rathenau, Spengler, Ortega y Gasset, and Huizinga, became widely spread in the first quarter of the century and since then has retained its grip upon our minds. It has been the central issue of many discussions in which leading philosophers and scientists of various nations have participated. The second conference of the Rencontres Internationales de Genève in 1947 was devoted to the theme "Progrès Technique et Progrès Moral." The title itself indicates that the identity of technological and human progress is no longer taken for granted. Two years later, at the Première Semaine Sociologique a group of French, American, and English sociologists and economists discussed similar problems, under the title "Industrialisation et Technocratie." In 1953 some of Germany's foremost intellectual leaders, including Romano Guardini, Werner Heisenberg, and Martin Heidegger, met in Munich for discussions exploring the relationship between art and technology.[6]

No attempt can be made here to describe these conferences or the huge general literature dealing with the relationship between technology and human values. We can only try to summarize briefly the essence of the arguments presented by those who take a pessimistic view concerning the impact of technological change. Technology, these skeptics tell us, has not fulfilled its promise to enable us to shape our own lives. Perhaps our work has become smoother and more efficient, but it has also become depersonalized. This depersonalization has turned into a dangerous force. Even our thinking and our living outside the work process have become largely standardized. Do we use our leisure time to express and develop those personal qualities which we are compelled to suppress while performing our work in factory, store, or office? Or do we prefer to evade the challenges which lie in the task of developing personal values and achieving wholeness of self? It may be painful to admit, but Hollywood producers are not wholly wrong when they emphasize the importance of standardized appeals and meet criticism of the low quality of their movies with the brutal reply: That's what the people like, and we give them what they want.

This trend toward depersonalization—the argument continues—reflects the innermost tendency of the machine age, leading away from the vital and organic and turning toward the mechanical and organized. Such a world of mechanization requires matter-of-factness as the prevailing attitude of mind. Life loses its quality of enchantment; nature no longer has mysteries but only problems. Everything, including man, has to become predictable and calculable. This unceasing process of calculation would be doomed to failure if it were confined to machines and materials and halted at the human person. Therefore individuals must be stripped of their individuality and treated as materials. It is not just a slip of the tongue when human beings are referred to as material in expressions such as "college material," "material for our clinics," and so on.[7]

Some critics of technology have emphasized that this depersonalization and matter-of-factness leads to an increasing insensitivity. Romano Guardini gives a striking illustration of the numbness of feeling which he considers a consequence of the machine age. In the past when one person killed another, a full and personal realization of his action could arise in him. But the situation is quite different when the killing is done "scientifically" from the distant height of an airplane. A button is pushed, and a hundred thousand persons are annihilated.[8]

All this is discouraging enough. But what makes the outlook of the critics even more despairing is their conviction that there is no way to fight or escape these trends toward depersonalization and mechanization. They believe that a tragic contradiction is inherent in the development of modern technology: the machine, created to serve the individual's purposes, has gained so much power that it has become immune to man's will. Instead of helping to implement the autonomy of the human being, the machine has triumphed over it. Technological development—though created by us—has emancipated itself from our direction and seems to follow its own inherent law. In our helplessness with respect to our own creation we have become like the sorcerer's apprentice who, looking with horror at the forces he has released but is unable to master, cries despairingly:

> Die ich rief, die Geister,
> Werd' ich nun nicht los.

> The Spirits that I summoned
> I cannot now dismiss.

Let us summarize these indictments of the machine age. Man can no longer express himself in his work. The increasing mechanization of life engenders a calculating outlook toward nature and society and dissolves the individual's bond of union with them. The world of machines follows its own course and escapes man's direction. These indictments culminate in the accusation that man in the technological age has become alienated from his work, from himself, and from the reality of society and nature. Such criticism is much more fundamental and comprehensive than the complaints of former times about isolated repercussions of expanding technology. It cannot be refuted with the arguments which were presented in the past in defence of the machine. In the eighteenth and nineteenth centuries it was pointed out that society was still at the beginning of technological development. Therefore men should not complain about a few painful experiences, but accept them as growing pains of a basically sound process, destined to disappear in the course of further evolution. What was needed was a readiness to put up with temporary sufferings, to face them with the determination: Forward to more technology. In our days this answer is no longer considered satisfactory, even by those who defend technology. The current defence is that the machine is essentially neutral and indifferent with respect to the ends it serves. It can be used for creative purposes or for destructive ones. It can help man to find himself or to become estranged from himself, to be closely related to the realities of nature and society or to be alienated from them. Therefore, the defence concludes, if you want to understand man's alienation don't look to technology. You will be more realistic if you concentrate on forces which by their very nature can't be neutral but grow out of conflict and the struggle for power. For example, why not examine the development of political institutions and their impact on man's existence?

CHAPTER THREE

Politics and Alienation

THERE SEEMS TO BE some evidence to support the view
that alienation is a rather recent phenomenon, largely
due to political developments of the last decades. It was
not until grave changes occurred in the regimes of various
European countries during the thirties of this century that
many of our contemporaries became aware for the first
time of the depersonalization of human lives and of forces
that turned individuals into mere objects. The fate of
hundreds of thousands of fleeing refugees in those dark
years has been powerfully expressed in Menotti's opera
The Consul. Stefan Zweig describes these experiences in
his memoirs *The World of Yesterday* in these words: "I
ceased to feel as if I quite belonged to myself. A part of
the natural identity with my original and essential ego
was destroyed forever. . . . If I reckon up the many forms
I have filled out during these years, declarations on every
trip, tax declarations, foreign exchange certificates, border
passes, entrance permits, departure permits, registrations
on coming and going; the many hours I have spent in
ante-rooms of consulates and officials, the many inspectors,

friendly and unfriendly, bored and overworked, before whom I have sat, the many examinations and interrogations at frontiers I have been through, then I feel keenly how much human dignity has been lost in this century which, in our youth, we had credulously dreamed of as one of freedom, as of the federation of the world. . . . When those of us who had once conversed about Baudelaire's poetry and spiritedly discussed intellectual problems met together, we would catch ourselves talking about affidavits and permits and whether one should apply for an immigration visa or a tourist visa; acquaintance with a stenographer in a consulate, who could cut down one's waiting-time was more significant to one's existence than friendship with a Toscanini or a Rolland. Human beings were made to feel that they were objects and not subjects, that nothing was their right but everything merely a favor by official grace."[1]

Many a reader will shrug his shoulders and say: This is finished now. We fought the greatest war in history to free humanity from the kind of suffering described by Zweig; and today, at least within the boundaries of the free world, man can be himself again. He is able to shape his life in accordance with his own choices and is no longer used as a tool for purposes which are alien to him. True—the supporters of this view will add—the size of our political communities and the intricacies of the problems of modern life make it impossible to allow the individual to have his say about all the decisions which must be taken. But even so, he can always make his voice heard; and the system of representation works in a way that ensures the basic identity of the will of the majority of private citizens with that of the governmental authorities. When this identity fails to appear, the estrangement between individuals and their representatives is not fundamental but only temporary. Situations of this kind result, not from the system of representation as such, but rather from improper functioning or inadequate development of democratic procedures.

This optimistic view seems to us not fully in agreement with reality. For even where the machinery designed to implement the democratic idea is working at its best and without interference on the part of special interest groups, where the right to vote is not limited by poll tax regulations, by arbitrary decisions on the part of registration boards, or by threats of violence by organized terror gangs, where the counting and announcement of election results is carried out correctly and fairly, there still remains in the minds of many citizens a strong awareness of a gulf between themselves and the elected governing bodies. We have only to remember the connotations inherent in terms like "politics" and "politicians" to realize how deeply many individuals feel themselves apart from the ways of thinking and acting of their political representatives. Political leaders, aware of this distance, have tried to overcome it. They attempt to establish a closer relationship to the public by proving themselves fighters for the common cause. Therefore they devote many efforts to building up issues which allegedly have grown out of the vital interests and needs of the people. Yet, much as these issues are dramatized by the leaders, the mass of individuals are sometimes embarrassingly slow in recognizing them as matters of *their* concern. This was illustrated by a public opinion survey conducted by Professor Samuel A. Stouffer of Harvard, a few years ago, of the problems which trouble Americans most. It showed that at the time of the Army-McCarthy hearings, when the dangers of subversion and conspiracy were being vividly described and appeared to worry deeply the man on the street, "less than 1% of the American public volunteered any concern about the internal Communist threat."[2]

Such artificiality in building up "issues" is sometimes drastically revealed. When radical organizations in this country speak up, for example, for members of racial minority groups who do not get fair court trials, their motives are often suspected. The question is raised as to whether they are moved by a genuine respect for human lives or by a tendency to play up an "issue" and to exploit it for their own political purposes. They are accused of losing all interest in the victims as soon as the latter can no longer be used to dramatize the political struggle waged by their defenders. Some experiences of the recent past seem to indicate that this pattern is not limited to fighters for radical causes. We have only to remember the fate of war prisoners who were welcomed as heroes in the days when their return to this country was considered a national issue, and a short time later were court-martialled and thrown into prison.

These observations don't imply that those who choose a political career are driven solely by a desire for power and are without sincere concern for the people they pretend to serve. Such an over-simplification would obscure the relationship between politics and alienation. Although numerous individuals who profess an interest in the cause of the people are really divorced from it and are only using it for their own personal ends and political careers, we should not ignore the many who dedicate themselves to political struggles because they identify themselves with the plight of their fellow men. Even they, however, in spite of their genuine motives, can easily become involved in situations or courses of action which are really alien to their purposes. The cause to which they are committed may encounter a resistance which cannot be broken except from a position of power. In the beginning this power may be sought, not for personal gain, but for the sake of ideas. However, many experiences from the past and from the contemporary scene seem to justify the pessimistic view that power in any form is tempting and that there is only a thin line of demarcation between power needed for political objectives and power coveted for personal ends. Becoming enamoured of personal power and feeling the desire to retain and expand it, the leader can easily grow apart from his followers and move away from his original purpose.

Even when power is not used for personal advantage, it often tends to widen the gulf between the champion of a political cause and his following. The leader will realize, for example, that his power is not yet sufficient to carry out his plans. Therefore he will decide to follow a course of give and take, to form alliances, to accept compromises—in brief, to play the game of *Realpolitik*. This forces him to sacrifice—temporarily, he thinks—some of the ideas which he had advocated in the days when he tried to win the masses to his cause. Although he may have taken all these steps in full integrity and in

the hope that they will help to prepare the ultimat
victory of his principles, his actions may be interpreted
quite differently and with growing suspicion by the rank
and file of his followers. Carefully designed measure
which grew out of the most cautious and minute planning
will appear as schemes and manipulations. Painful de
cisions to accept unsatisfactory but strategically necessar
compromises will be misjudged as resulting from un
principled opportunism, as betraying the originally pro
claimed ideal. This criticism may be mistaken and unfai
with regard to the motives to which it ascribes the leader'
actions. Yet it will be hard to silence it and to ignore th
human dilemma which those who devote their lives t
political movements and struggles frequently have to face

Max Weber, a few weeks before his death, gave
gripping speech in which he described the tragedy inheren
in the fight for a political cause. It was the period after th
German monarchy had collapsed, when, perhaps for th
first time in the history of Germany, a large number o
students and of the younger generation demanded th
liquidation of militarism and power politics. Webe
strongly opposed the belief of the "pacifist utopians" wh
dreamed of a world in which dealings of one governmen
with another one were to be guided by the same ethica
principles which private individuals are supposed t
follow. With great passion he rejected the demand t
eliminate the difference between private and politica
morality. He believed this demand to be based on an en
tirely false concept of the relationship between means an
ends, on the erroneous assumption that from good wil
come only good, from evil only evil. Against this optimisti

simplification Weber emphasized the heterogeneous relationship between means and ends, which is ignored by those who are unable to face the "ethical irrationality" of this world and who try to escape from the truth that the world is full of devils. He who enters politics, that is, the realm where power and ruthlessness alone are valid means, concludes a pact with diabolic forces. Condemning any statesman who hesitates to use unethical means in the pursuit of his ends, Weber takes a strong stand in favor of Machiavelli and admiringly quotes this author's praise for citizens who put the greatness of their commonwealth above the salvation of their souls.[3]

Many of us may question Weber's views, which seem to have been influenced by his own religious position and his belief in the role of the forces of evil in this world. We may reject his idea that the realm of political decision and the realm of ethics are inherently and by their very nature opposed to each other, that the conflict between them is essentially irreconcilable. We will have to admit, however, that in our age many statesmen, facing the dilemma which Weber has described, have become alienated, not only from their followers and their objectives, but even from their inner selves.

Our period is not the first to see the tragic plight of great leaders and statesmen. More than one hundred years ago Hegel described the fate of those who, chosen by history to become the executors of its will, have fulfilled the task that was their destiny: "When their object is attained they fall off like empty hulls from the kernel. They die early like Alexander; they are murdered like Caesar; transported to St. Helena, like Napoleon."[4] Hegel

51

emphasized the misfortune of the political leader *after* he had achieved his mission. Today we are aware that even in the days when the leader is still in the midst of his struggles he is subject to the unhappy fate of the alienated man.

If political leaders who are in a position of power find it so hard to be themselves, we can imagine that the plight of a great many members of the political community is even more difficult. In March 1953, Robert C. Storey, then President of the American Bar Association, gave a speech in Washington in which he called the residents of the United States "the most lawless people in the world" and challenged them to awaken "to the enormity of this problem."[5] Every year hundreds of articles are written, and many television and radio programs are presented, describing the inner decay of American life caused by a disturbing increase in crime, in political graft, in corruption of law enforcing agencies, by the changing moral standards of the young as evidenced by sad experiences at schools (even at such high ranking ones as West Point), by developments in the field of college athletics, and so on. Well aware that a crisis of this scope and kind cannot be overcome by moralizing denunciations of the secular and materialistic spirit of our age or by well meaning pleas for more civic-mindedness, many individuals and groups advocate a more "scientific" approach to this phenomenon of social disintegration. Thus numerous study groups and research projects serving this purpose have been put into operation during recent years.

In the past, Americans, when faced with difficult situations, suggested hopefully, "Let's have a law." Now they seem inclined to add, "Let's have a study." About four years ago, after the discovery of an atrocious crime committed by four Brooklyn boys, the head of a well-known public relations firm published a letter in which he offered to finance an extensive psychiatric study of the motives of this "shockingly aberrant" behavior. He expressed the almost pathetic hope that such research might "do for our society, in this field, what comparable studies have done in other fields, for instance, the Hoover reorganization study for our government, the Flexner study for medical education, and so on."[6]

As much as systematic inquiries into the causes of current maladjustments in society are needed, many of them do not really enrich our understanding. Adopting methods which have proven themselves useful in the natural sciences, they start by defining their subject in a very specialized way and concentrate on some detailed problem—the impact of radio and television programs, of comic books and movies, on juvenile delinquency; the social implications of slum conditions or of the influx of new ethnic groups into previously homogeneous neighborhoods; the effects of overprotective child care, of authoritarian and permissive methods, in education; the emotional adjustment of middle class and underprivileged children from broken homes; the relative increase in homicide rates in urban and rural communities; the relationship between social status and divorce rate, between unemployment and alcoholism, between addiction to drugs and sex perversion, between premarital pregnancy and the divorce rate; the comparative rates of recidivism among racial minority and majority groups; and so on. Studies of this kind, dealing with some special aspect of social malad-justment, recommend themselves because they proceed by gathering a large quantity of empirical data. Such a factual approach seems to free us from the abstract dogmas held by those who theorize about the relationship of society as a whole to the development of crime. Let us ask, how-ever, whether the concentration on partial aspects of the problem is really as divorced from preconceived ideas as it appears to be. Could it not be that in collecting and observing the many factual details which are expected to throw light on specific questions, the investigators are guided by certain tacit premises as, for example, the as-sumption that our society is fundamentally sound and that therefore its disturbances do not emanate from inner tendencies but from abnormal and extraneous develop-ments?[7] We are not questioning here the validity of such an assumption, but merely state that it *is* an assumption. By its very nature it focuses from the outset exclusively on some special sector of our social institutions, not even raising the question as to whether there might be a con-nection between the basic character of modern society and the present trend toward lawlessness.

As a first approach to this larger question, let us con-sider Malcolm Cowley's recent description of "a general literary movement that seems to be dominant everywhere in Western literature: a movement from sociology to psychology, from political to personal problems, in a word, from the public to the private."[8] It would be entirely wrong to consider this tendency to retreat from the public as a trend limited to literature. The extent to which it permeates our society has been shown recently in the

public opinion survey mentioned above. This survey regis-
tered the answers of a cross-section of Americans to the
question "What kinds of things do you worry about
most?" Reporting on the findings of the study Dr. Stouffer
states: "An overwhelming majority answered *solely* in
terms of personal or family problems (health, finances,
employment, children's welfare, etc.); 43% were worried
about health—their own or of someone in the family.
Only 8% were worried about world problems, including
the shadow of war. And of these 8% a great many were
concerned for strictly personal reasons—the possibility of
being drafted or having a son drafted."[9]

Even those who are directly affected by the great
struggles of our age and whose very lives are at stake often
fail to overcome the inner distance toward the issues for
which they fight on the battlefield. During the Korean
War the G.I.s liked to sing a song called "The Dear John
Letter." It does not mention one word about the cause for
which our boys were called to arms but reveals only the
personal story of the soldier who receives a letter from
his bride-to-be. She has found it too long to wait for his
return and has therefore given her heart to another man,
whom she plans to marry the next weekend. He happens
to be the G.I.'s brother.

There may be many reasons why only a small number
of people seem to be concerned about problems of public
life. Whatever our interpretation may be, there remains
the fact that in a period in which we are constantly re-
minded that our nation faces very crucial decisions, that
its very life is at stake, personal questions appear to be
the only ones that matter to us. Thus the movement from

55

political to personal problems, from the public to the private, of which Malcolm Cowley spoke is not confined to literature. It reflects the contemporary situation of man. Increasingly he senses a split between his existence as an individual and as a citizen: he finds himself powerless to integrate these two roles, which he has come to see as separate and often conflicting parts of his life. The awareness of this rift indicates the extent to which man has become divorced from the political community.

Where this alienation prevails, civic-mindedness ceases to be a real force. Although it does not disappear altogether, it is practiced only by a few dedicated idealists or becomes a kind of afterthought on the part of individuals who are successful in the pursuit of their private interests but still remember a certain obligation toward less fortunate members of the community. We should not overlook the significance of these vestiges of public spirit. But at the same time we should be aware that they are not sufficient to counteract the dominant trend toward a dangerous decline of civic-mindedness.

When this disintegration of public morale has once started, the political community has lost its lifeblood. No longer is there any genuine concern for its welfare and its needs, no longer is there an *inner* respect for its legal order. Fear of punishment, often derided as the timidity of the coward and "sissy," has become the only force to maintain the semblance of a lawful society. Thus man's alienation from his political community has done more to engender the present state of lawlessness than all the special factors analyzed in the scientific studies mentioned above.

It is true that alienation brought about by political trends is a process which has been going on for a long time. It did not start in our present period, but its manifestations have become so striking and so widely spread that we are now increasingly aware of it. We need only think of the experiences of American soldiers and their families during the Korean War to realize how many people find their fate shaped by forces which reach from the outside into their lives and with which they have no inner relationship. Although only some eight years lie between the return of World War II and Korean War soldiers, a striking difference between the two groups of veterans has been noticed by many observers. It has been well described in an article called "Portrait of the Korean Veteran."[10] George Barrett, the author, who was for two years in Korea as a reporter for the *New York Times* and who after his return spent much time in studying the attitudes and problems of the G.I.s after they had been discharged, checked his impressions with those of experts in veterans' affairs. The picture he draws shows the ex-soldier as disoriented as he was in Korea. His extreme "unconnectedness" reveals itself in his complete lack of any feeling that those who have gone through similar army experiences, or have served in the same unit, are his pals. Barrett describes a situation in which one of the interviewers finds out with some surprise that the Korean veteran before him has belonged to the same Army outfit in which he himself went over to the European war theater some years earlier: " 'The Second Division' he exclaims. He puts the record down. 'You know, there's an Indian-head patch on one of my khakis yet. I was at Eisenborn—Battle of the Bulge. The Second's still taking on the dirty details, I see.' The Korean veteran looks up, says politely to the man who is eight years his senior: 'Yes sir.' That's all." This aloofness, Barrett seems to think, is nothing new for the Korean veteran. It came over him when he was still in Korea, unable to understand, not only the war, but above all his *participation* in it. When he asked himself why he was in this fight he could only answer with the one sentence which, according to Barrett, became the standard phrase among Korean G.I.s, repeated over and over again to indicate the utter meaninglessness of life: "That's the way the ball bounces." It would be wrong to trace this remoteness from the purpose of the war to the fears of the soldier who lacks combat experience. Barrett quotes the words of a first lieutenant who had been in World War II and who later on completed fifty-one missions of night combat in Korea: "Maybe it's because war has become impersonalized more than ever, maybe it's because when we were flying combat over Europe we saw towns and even lights, but in Korea we'd be flying at night and there was nothing to see, and suddenly we'd realize that we were alone, and we'd say to ourselves in real disbelief, 'My God, what am I doing here?' "

Many of us are inclined to blame the government or military agencies for the soldiers' lack of understanding of their part in the Korean War. A systematic and intensified orientation program carried out on a large-scale basis—we may think—would have enabled the soldier to grasp the meaning of the Korean conflict. In all fairness to the responsible authorities, it must be said that they fully recognized the need for building up such programs and that they tried to do everything in their power to make them as effective as possible. "An impressive library of books," Barrett writes at the end of his article, "could be made up of the tons of paper used by generals and admirals and public information specialists and visiting Congressmen trying to explain the reasons for the Korean War to the guy fighting it. But he didn't get it. And he still doesn't."

An inquiry into the relationship between alienation and politics cannot help presenting trends which are disheartening. We see bureaucratic agencies treat man as a mere object. We see some political leaders build up issues in order to manipulate the thoughts of the masses, and others discover that only by sacrificing their principles and turning to a game of *Realpolitik* can they attain the power they deem necessary in the pursuit of their political aims. We see a large number of people, finding it impossible to integrate their roles as private individuals and as citizens, either defy the law or follow it, not out of inner respect for the needs of the community, but only out of fear of punishment. We see soldiers fight in a war which they are unable to understand and to which they are so inwardly indifferent that they can only account for their participation with the completely fatalistic words "That's the way the ball bounces." When we witness all these tendencies to which man's estrangement from his political community has led, we can easily be overpowered by feelings of sadness about the present and hopelessness about the future. At this stage of our study we shall not attempt to decide whether this pessimistic outlook is justified, or whether there are forces at work (or at least dormant) which may succeed in counteracting the menace of disintegration. Both those who have given in to a gloomy view of the future and those who cling to a more hopeful outlook normally base their arguments on the premise that man's alienation and the ensuing crisis of our public life have been brought about by political forces. This, however, is an unproven assumption. To state that there is a link between man's estrangement from his political community and the present decay of our public life does not establish a causal relationship and does not prove that political developments have engendered man's alienation. Nothing that has been said in the preceding inquiry indicates that man's estrangement, which makes itself *felt* in the political life of today, actually *results* from it. Before deciding this question, let us look at the socio-economic framework within which our political institutions operate. It is there that some outstanding social scientists, particularly in the past, have believed they discovered the basis of modern man's alienation.

CHAPTER FOUR

Social Structure and Alienation

SOCIOLOGICAL WORK in the United States and in many European countries has lost much of its self-assurance in recent years. The hope that sociology will one day acquire the reliability of a strict science has not been completely abandoned, but it is no longer as widely held. More qualifications are made now concerning the claim that social sciences ought to follow methods and procedures which have been developed and applied successfully in the natural sciences. This tendency toward a more cautious attitude can be noticed in discussions on the question of measurement in sociology. There are scholars who, for theoretical reasons, have taken a negative stand from the outset and have long challenged the validity and the relevancy of quantifying methods in treating sociological questions. But even those who have accepted this methodological approach in principle and have actively engaged in its application now show a growing awareness of the need for re-examining the concept of measurement in sociology.[1]

This growing reservation in regard to quantifying

61

procedures so far does not seem to have appreciably affected the prevailing pattern of sociological research work. Nevertheless it is important because it is one of many manifestations of a larger trend. There are numerous indications of an increasing recognition that a reappraisal and reorientation of contemporary sociological thinking have become necessary. This need has been emphasized by many authors, including T. H. Marshall, Christopher Dawson, Robert S. Lynd, Jules Monnerot, Behice Boran, Herbert Blumer, Robert Redfield, Edward A. Shils, Howard Becker, Reinhard Bendix, and Florian Znaniecki.[2] All these writers express a certain disillusionment with the prevailing orientation of sociological thought. They differ in regard to the diagnosis of the malady, but quite a few of them seem to agree with the explanation given by Znaniecki. In his presidential address at the 1954 meeting of the American Sociological Society, he focused on "the most serious defect of our systematic sociological theories, a defect which goes back to Auguste Comte." He referred to the antithesis which is so often set up between "social statics" and "social dynamics," or in more recent terminology, between "social structure" and "social change." In criticizing the lack of coordination between these two ways of viewing social phenomena, Znaniecki stated: "Many textbooks include a number of chapters about social structures and then separate chapters about social changes. Some books deal almost exclusively with social structure; others exclusively with social change."[3]

There are many who accept the separation between the static and dynamic approaches without question. They defend the differentiation as a methodological device, to which no objection can be raised as long as the findings, separately arrived at, are brought together later on. It is hard to accept this argument as valid. Structure and change are interwoven in the fabric of social phenomena, and their basic oneness is the core of social reality. Therefore we see little promise in a method which starts out to isolate the elements of statics and dynamics and subsequently tries to piece them together by an additive procedure.

Moreover it is doubtful whether methodological considerations are the main reason for the situation described by Znaniecki. In our view the unrelatedness of studies on social structures and on social change results largely from the way the relationship between sociology and history is conceived in contemporary social sciences. Most contemporary sociological work reveals a non-historical, or even anti-historical, orientation. This trend has often been described as an understandable revolt against the legacy of the nineteenth century, when, under the influence of Comte and the great systematizers, sociologists envisaged the theory of society largely as a philosophy of history.

There is no doubt today that the premises of the early nineteenth century sociological systems are no longer valid and that we must redefine the relationship between sociology and history. But do we meet this challenge by the radical separation of sociological and historical analysis which has become the prevailing procedure in sociology? Such a division dominates that part of sociological work which tries to understand social structures divorced from, and independent of, their historical foundations and settings. It characterizes also that part of sociological work which concerns itself with social dynamics. Inquiries into social change have accumulated huge amounts of data about trends in certain fields—the age distribution of the U.S. population, the ethnic composition of neighborhood communities, food habits, standards of sexual behavior, and so on. Valuable as many of these studies are, they have so far concentrated on *changes* occurring in particular and isolated fields. They have shied away from studying the basic pattern of our social world, from envisaging contemporary society as a whole in the perspective of *change*.

Many believe that this omission is only due to fortuitous circumstances—such as the high degree of specialization in the social sciences or their tendency to react against the tradition of nineteenth century sociology. It can be asked, however, whether the failure to apply the concept of change to present-day society as a whole does not reflect a more basic attitude. A feeling of uncertainty about the future makes it hard for many of us, including the social scientist, to view the present as part of an historical process and as such subject to change, not only in isolated aspects, but at its very core.[4]

Whatever the answer to this question may be, the separation of the social from the historical which now prevails represents, in our opinion, a serious obstacle to the effort to arrive at a sociological understanding of the fundamental trends of our period. This belief has prompted us to begin our inquiry into the relationship between society and the forces of alienation with the help of a sociological concept which focuses on society as a historical process: the theory developed by Ferdinand Tönnies in his *Gemeinschaft und Gesellschaft*.

Thinkers whose insights move ahead of their age have to pay the price of loneliness. Ferdinand Tönnies went through this experience. His life as a scholar and the fate of *Gemeinschaft und Gesellschaft* tell the story of years of isolation. When this work, which eventually became one of the deepest influences on sociological thought, was first published in 1887 it remained almost unnoticed. Not only the general public but many of the leading minds of the period failed to grasp its significance.[5] The author remained relatively unknown, and his academic success was quite moderate for a long time. Only a few students were attracted to the courses he offered; and nearly thirty years went by before he was offered a professorship.

Twenty-five years went by before a second edition of *Gemeinschaft und Gesellschaft* was published in 1912. A few years later, when in the growing mood of skepticism that followed World War I the idea of progress was severely challenged, there was a sudden awakening of interest in Tönnies' thought. *Gemeinschaft und Gesellschaft* was "discovered" almost overnight, and many new editions were necessary within a period of a few years. Tönnies, however, who had never been concerned about career or success, was unimpressed by this startling change and soon grew uneasy about the sudden acclaim. He realized that beneath it was the same tendency to revolt against the age of science, technology, and rationalism which made people turn to Spengler's sensational *Decline of the West*. Thoroughly uncomfortable in the company of the literati who tried to escape from the challenge of contemporary society, he withdrew from those who were trying to make *Gemeinschaft und Gesellschaft* fashionable.

Thus the scholar found himself alone again, almost as alone as he had been in the days when his work had been ignored.

What is the content of this book which has had such a changing fate? Any attempt to summarize it meets with considerable linguistic difficulty, since a satisfactory translation of the terms *Gemeinschaft* and *Gesellschaft* has never been proposed and in our view cannot be found. Therefore we have decided not to present definitional formulas but to describe the meaning of the two concepts.

Tönnies believes that a distinction should be made between two essentially different bases of human association. The one which he calls *Gesellschaft* is a relationship contractual in its nature, deliberately established by individuals who realize that they cannot pursue their proper interests effectively in isolation and therefore band together. The other, named *Gemeinschaft*, is a social unit which does not primarily come into being through conscious design: one finds oneself belonging to it as one belongs to one's home. Individuals who enter a *Gesellschaft* do so with only a fraction of their being, that is, with that part of their existence which corresponds to the specific purpose of the organization. Members of a taxpayer's association, or individuals who own stock in a company, are related to each other, not as whole persons, but with only that part of themselves which is concerned with being a taxpayer or shareholder. They leave out, or are supposed to leave out, of their association all the other qualities which constitute their lives—their family background, their friendships and hatreds, their religious beliefs, political loyalties, and so on. Thus they remain loosely connected and essentially remote from each other. Very different is the association called *Gemeinschaft*. It does not come into being through planning and conscious organization. Its members are bound to each other as whole persons rather than as fragmentary individuals. The purest form of *Gemeinschaft* is within the family, particularly in the relation between mother and child, where unity is the first stage in development and separation is a later phase. In the *Gemeinschaft* unity prevails, in spite of occasional separation; in the *Gesellschaft* separation prevails, in spite of occasional unity.[6]

So deep is the separation between man and man in *Gesellschaft* that "everybody is by himself and isolated, and there exists a condition of tension against all others." Thus *Gesellschaft* becomes a social world in which latent hostility and potential war are inherent in the relationship of one to another.[7]

In terms of historical development, Tönnies holds that society has moved away from an age where *Gemeinschaft* was predominant towards an age where *Gesellschaft* prevails. This process of transition, which started many centuries ago, was accelerated by changes begun during the Renaissance and particularly by those resulting from the Industrial Revolution. It is a transformation which is inexorable and which we cannot evade. No use to lament, as some romanticists do, the increasing mechanization of human relations in modern society. The process which brings about the steady yielding of *Gemeinschaft* to *Gesellschaft* seems to be our fate. No escape or return to *Gemeinschaft* is possible.

There is something disturbing about Tönnies' idea

67

that we must resign ourselves to living in a depersonalized world, in an age of *Gesellschaft*. In recent years some American sociologists, including Morris Janowitz, Daniel Bell, and Edward A. Shils, have criticised those who are preoccupied with "the one-way trend from *Gemeinschaft* to *Gesellschaft*" and have emphasized that this development is not irreversible. It is argued that modern society has given rise to many associations which have the character of *Gemeinschaft* and that Americans, especially, are members of numerous organizations, clubs, lodges, fraternities, and so on. Those who present this argument often fail to ask whether the very need for "joining" is not indicative of the isolation felt by individuals who live in an atomized society. Moreover, they focus primarily on the large *quantity* of societies into which contemporary men enter and neglect to consider the *quality* of relations predominating in these organizations. It should not be taken for granted that every club has the characteristics of a *Gemeinschaft*. Disparities between the avowed objectives of an organization and its actual functioning often arise. The character of *Gemeinschaft* which appears as the facade of many groups is frequently nothing but an appearance. *Pseudo-Gemeinschaft*, to use a term coined by Robert K. Merton, is a widely spread phenomenon.[8]

It is not hard to understand why so many individuals protest against the idea that the age of *Gemeinschaft* has passed. As much as we try to tell ourselves that we can't turn the clock back, we find it hard to accept a trend which seems to impoverish our lives and to deprive us of the sense of belonging for which most of us yearn. As we like to look back to the days of a warm and sheltered childhood, so we tend to hark back to the past of our society when the bonds of *Gemeinschaft* were still strong and protected those whom they enfolded. Tönnies had a sympathetic understanding of this tendency to look back to times which had gone by. Yet he clearly saw the dangers lying in such an orientation, and emphasized that to cherish our past does not mean that we should try to return to it.

As Marx warned that a man cannot become a child again unless he becomes childish, so Tönnies saw great dangers in the attempt to restore forms of *Gemeinschaft* which had lost their meaning in the modern world. These efforts, he feared, could produce only artificial facades, empty forms, which instead of serving the forces of life and furthering their growth would stifle and destroy them. Tönnies' fears were borne out in a tragic way in the thirties when Hitler and his followers, imbued with their idea of national *Gemeinschaft*, attempted to reverse the direction in which German life was moving. Instead of harking back to an age which has passed, instead of nurturing the illusion that we can restore *Gemeinschaft* at will, we should learn—Tönnies urges us—to accept the trend toward *Gesellschaft* as our fate and to face up to the challenge with which this situation confronts us. When we no longer shy away from these tasks but try to fulfill them, we may hope that life will go on, that the constructive energies which lie beneath the age of *Gesellschaft* will unfold and eventually lead to the rise of a new stage of society in which higher forms of *Gesellschaft* and *Gemeinschaft* can be developed and integrated with each other.

Methodological considerations lead Tönnies in some

of his studies to separate sociological questions from those of individual psychology. Yet he is always aware of the artificial character of such a differentiation and never loses sight of the extent to which mind and society are intertwined. He is especially interested in the interplay between the transition from *Gemeinschaft* to *Gesellschaft* and the changing direction of the human mind and will. This is the subject of the second section of his book, which is entitled "Natural Will and Rational Will." Parallel with his differentiation between *Gemeinschaft* and *Gesellschaft*, Tönnies distinguishes between two forms of human will. The first, which he calls *Wesenwille* (the word has been translated "natural will" or "integral will"), is impulsive. It is a spontaneous expression of man's drives and desires, of his natural disposition. The second, which the author calls *Kürwille*, is primarily shaped by the deliberative processes of the rational mind. It lacks the qualities of spontaneity and impulsiveness which sustain *Wesenwille*. It admits only decisions which result from a cautious assessment of all the pros and cons and from prudent choosing between them. (The first part of the word *Kürwille* is derived from the old German verb *Küren* which means to choose.) *Wesenwille* is "the will which includes the thinking"; *Kürwille* is "the thinking which encompasses the will."[9]

Individuals in whom *Wesenwille* is predominant show a quality of directness in their character. Their personalities seem to be of one piece and animate all their actions. Such a oneness is lost when *Kürwille* prevails. Objectives are pursued, not because they emanate from an inner necessity and mean personal fulfillment, but because well-weighed considerations have proven them advantageous. Conclusions of this kind are reached only after sober calculation, especially of the probable costs to be incurred and their ratio to the anticipated results. The awareness of means and ends as two separate and independent categories is the very core of *Kürwille,* whereas both are blended and remain undifferentiated in *Wesenwille.*

To illustrate this difference between *Wesenwille* and *Kürwille* we first choose an example from the realm of human work. In a previous chapter we described the condemnation of the machine which is expressed today by so many individuals and groups. Much as we may reject these accusations levelled at the technological age, we cannot dispute the fact that the work of many people— and not only of those who are subject to the monotony of the assembly line—has become depersonalized to a very high degree. The satisfaction which most of us find in our work is not inherent in the occupational activities which we have to carry out; it is found primarily in the pay envelope which is handed to us as the equivalent for the number of hours put in. Thus work is not done for its own sake but for an extrinsic end. Work of this kind requires a society in which man has learned to differentiate between means and ends, to avail himself of means which have no inner relationship to his life and its goals and which he *chooses* to use because he has figured out the advantages they are likely to yield. It can be performed only where man's activities are directed by the calculations of *Kürwille.*

The critical reader might answer that the split between means and ends is the very essence of work, that the impetus to work can only emanate from *Kürwille* and

71

never from *Wesenwille*. This argument does not appear valid to us. In our opinion it is based on a tendency to narrow the concept of work and to focus too exclusively on specific manifestations of the work life in modern business civilization. Even today work patterns can be found which have little in common with the depersonalized activities of *Kürwille* and to which the above described differentiation between means and ends does not apply. We like to think of the work of the devoted priest, of the great creative artist, or of the inspiring educator as different from those occupations which people engage in primarily to earn their livelihood. Turning to earlier stages of human civilization, we are unwilling to accept the romantic idealization of the past which glosses over the crudity and drudgery of men's living conditions in the ages before the Industrial Revolution. Yet we will have to recognize that work in those bygone periods, far from necessitating the abandonment of personal impulses and attitudes, was an avenue for their expression and fulfillment. It had little in common with the impersonal activities of modern "economic man," with his tendency to separate means and ends. J. A. Hobson, the British economist, has described the development of early crafts in a few sentences which also apply to the nature of activities prompted by *Wesenwille*. He notices that "even in those early handicrafts devoted to the most practical needs of life, the decorative instinct generally finds expression. Not only the weapons of the men, but the pots and pans and other domestic utensils of the women, carry carvings or mouldings, which testify to the play of art impulses. Leisure and pleasure thus appear as ingredients in the earliest industries." The author ends his exposition by saying that "we everywhere find what we call distinctively economic motives and activities almost inextricably intertwined, or even fused, with other motives and activities, sportive, artistic, religious, social and political."[10]

We add a second example to illustrate the difference between *Wesenwille* and *Kürwille*. It concerns the motives which prompt people to associate with each other. *Kürwille* directs us to choose the company of individuals toward whom we don't necessarily feel drawn. It may even lead us to suppress or conceal our dislikes, because we realize that it is useful to know the right people and to cultivate "friendship" with them. Thus in personal relations as in work *Kürwille* divorces means and ends. It makes us use human beings as tools for purposes which are not inherent in them but are devised by us.

Wesenwille, on the other hand, leads to a very different kind of human relations. Individuals who are primarily guided by it find difficulty in overcoming their likes and dislikes. They do not associate with others because as cautious strategists they have figured out that it is useful to be "good mixers" and to choose the right, that is, influential, acquaintances. Instead they feel a strong attachment and a genuine closeness to the persons with whom they make friends.

From our remarks on the different kinds of human relations engendered by *Kürwille* and *Wesenwille* it can be seen that an affinity exists between *Wesenwille* and *Gemeinschaft,* on the one hand, and between *Kürwille* and *Gesellschaft* on the other. In Tönnies' words, *Wesenwille* carries the conditions for *Gemeinschaft* and *Kürwille*

73

develops *Gesellschaft*.[11] As *Gemeinschaft* embraces all aspects of its members' lives, *Wesenwille* and its manifestations embody and express the whole of a person's being. On the other hand as individuals join a *Gesellschaft* only with a segment of their existence, so where *Kürwille* prevails their lives become subdivided and compartmentalised. This correlation between *Gemeinschaft* and *Wesenwille* and between *Gesellschaft* and *Kürwille* is important for grasping Tönnies' thinking on the historical sequence between the two forms of will. Since he sees history as leading from an age of *Gemeinschaft* toward an age of *Gesellschaft*, he also sees it as proceeding from *Wesenwille* to *Kürwille*. In particular he believes that the modern period can be understood only when the triumph of the forces of *Gesellschaft* and *Kürwille* is recognized.

This point is vividly expressed in Tönnies' account of Hobbes's age as a time when people started to break away from tradition and prevailing patterns of thought. "Man still has his center in his family, in his community and in his social estate [that is, the status group to which he and his family belong]. Monetary economy is still weak and therefore individual ownership has not yet reached an acute stage. Slowly, in a process which is often impeded and interrupted, further development erodes these conditions. Feelings and ideas which prevailed heretofore, begin to change. The individual centered on himself and what belongs to him [Tönnies alludes here to the book *Der Einzige und sein Eigenthum* written by the extreme individualist Max Stirner] increasingly becomes the predominant type of man in society. He thinks, he

74

calculates, he reckons his advantage. To him everything becomes a means to an end. Notably his relationship to other men, and thus to associations of all kinds, begins to change. He dissolves and concludes pacts and alliances according to his interests, i.e. as means to his ends. Although he finds it difficult to extricate himself from certain relationships into which he was born, he reflects on their usefulness and in his thoughts, at least, makes them dependent on his will."[12]

Some readers will see in this description of modern man and his social world a parallel to David Riesman's interpretation of the situation of the individual living in a social order which is not any longer tradition-directed. Riesman's views are much in line with those of Tönnies when he writes: ". . . the greatest social and characterological shift of recent centuries did indeed come when men were driven out of the primary ties that bound them to the western medieval version of tradition-directed society. . . . All later shifts, including the shift from inner-direction to other-direction, seem unimportant by comparison."[13] Riesman's book is an important contribution to the understanding of the contemporary social scene and its impact on personality structures. Against the background of the historical development described by Tönnies it will appear, however, that the inner-directed man and the other-directed man, in spite of the many differences and contrasts between them, do not represent absolute opposites but are kindred in spirit. Both were created by the movement which led to the victory of *Gesellschaft* over *Gemeinschaft* and to the rise of men primarily directed by *Kürwille*. The glad-hand strategies pursued by the seemingly "people-minded" other-directed man should not make us overlook that essentially he remains separated from his fellow men and in this regard is not very different from his counterpart, the inner-directed man.

By connecting the change from *Gemeinschaft* to *Gesellschaft* with the transition from *Wesenwille* to *Kürwille* Tönnies' work combines psychology and sociology in an original way. This is the contribution which Höffding, the Danish philosopher, emphasized as one of the essential features of *Gemeinschaft und Gesellschaft* when in 1890 he wrote one of the first reviews of the book.[14] Yet it is also a feature of Tönnies' thought which has been misunderstood. His work has been sometimes described as an attempt to reduce social processes and structures to psychological ones.[15] This interpretation, which we consider incorrect, may have been provoked by some of the author's own formulations—for example, the statement that "*Wesenwille* carries the conditions for *Gemeinschaft* and *Kürwille* develops *Gesellschaft.*" Such a statement, taken out of context, might easily lead us to overlook Tönnies' fundamental contention that the forces of society and the individual's will act and react on one another. He treats them throughout his book as two inter-related parts of one whole; and wherever the development of his ideas requires a stronger focus on one of the two aspects, he admits the relative incompleteness of his exposition. "Since this book," he states at the end of Book Two of *Gemeinschaft und Gesellschaft,* "starts from individual psychology, there is lacking the complementary but opposing view which describes how *Gemeinschaft* develops and fosters natural will (*Wesenwille*), on the one hand, and, on the other, binds and hinders rational will (*Kürwille*). The approach does not describe how *Gesellschaft* not only frees rational will but also requires and furthers it, even makes its unscrupulous use in competition into a condition of the maintenance of the individual, thus destroying the flowering and fruition of the natural will. Thus, adjusting to the conditions of *Gesellschaft* and imitating such actions of others as lead to gain and profits are not only the results of a natural drive, but such action becomes imperative and failure to conform is punishable under pain of destruction."[16]

This statement is a clear rejection of any attempt to oversimplify the relationship between sociology and psychology by reducing social structures to emotional ones. More than that, it indicates that Tönnies, in describing the role of *Kürwille* in the life of modern man and in developing the theory of *Gesellschaft*, has used as his point of departure the socio-economic processes dominating contemporary capitalist society. "In presenting the process of *Gesellschaft*," he wrote about thirteen years after the publication of his book, "the author has had in mind *modern* society and in doing so he has made due use of Karl Marx's disclosure of its economic law of motion, as the informed reader will easily notice and as has been explicitly acknowledged in the Preface of the book."[17]

There is indeed a considerable affinity between Marx's theory of capitalist economy and Tönnies' concept of *Gesellschaft*, a fact of which Tönnies was very much aware. In the Preface to the first edition of *Gemeinschaft und Gesellschaft* (written in February 1887) Tönnies points to three "outstanding authors" whose works have had a decisive impact on his thinking. He lists Sir Henry Maine and Otto Gierke, and after commenting on the latter's scholarly achievements he states that he missed in Gierke's view the economic orientation which had already become "extremely important" for him. He then adds the name of the third writer, Karl Marx, whom he characterizes as "the most remarkable and profound social philosopher precisely in regard to the development of this economic perspective." The idea which dominates *Gemeinschaft und Gesellschaft,* he believes, is not strange to the historians Maine and Gierke "although only the author who first penetrated the capitalist method of production could succeed in developing and clarifying it."[18] While rejecting political radicalism and all attempts to change the social order by acts of violence, Tönnies persisted throughout his life in his esteem for Marx's theoretical work. Even in those of his writings which present objections to some Marxian views he does not adopt the attitude of many of his colleagues who feel themselves called upon to refute Marxism. In his book *Marx: Leben und Lehre* (Marx: Life and Teachings), which was written from a critical point of view, he does not hesitate to acknowledge the agreement between his theory of *Gesellschaft* and the description of the relationship between individual and society which Marx presents in his famous essays on the Jewish question. And although Tönnies tries to prove the incorrectness of some of Marx's positions, he is ready to reiterate the indebtedness to Marx which he had expressed forty-two years before, at the time when he published *Gemeinschaft und Gesellschaft.* "I can't say," he writes in the Preface, "that I have learned or unlearned enough since that time to revise my judgement about Marx and his importance to any extent." He ends the book with the statement: "Marx, notwithstanding the deficiencies which adhere to his work and his performance, will maintain his rank as an epoch-making man and thinker through the centuries."[19]

The closeness between Marx's and Tönnies' views reaches beyond the authors' sociological theories. Tönnies often expressed his basic agreement with the tenets of the economic interpretation of history, although he cautioned against the danger of oversimplifying its statements, particularly against the misconception that only the modes of economic production are real while developments of the "superstructure"—for example, the legal, political, or artistic processes—have no reality of their own. Tönnies believes that this misunderstanding is not solely the result of dogmatic pronouncements on the part of overzealous disciples. Marx himself invited an erroneous interpretation by some of his own formulations, particularly by the way he used the expression "the real foundation" in describing the basic importance of the economic structure of society. In the Preface to the *Critique of Political Economy* Marx summed up his views on the relationship between economic institutions and the development of ideas by choosing the architectural image of foundation and superstructure. Tönnies regards this analogy as unfortunate and prefers the formulation in Marx's statement at the beginning of his discussion, that ideas are rooted in the economic conditions of life. It is obvious, Tönnies adds, that one cannot consider a tree as fictitious and only its roots as real.[20]

His awareness of the great significance of economic forces guides Tönnies in his analysis of the development of contemporary world politics. He traces the imperialism of the leading countries to the increased competition of various capital groups on the world market, to trade interests, and to the incessant tendency of capitalist enterprise to increase surplus value. At the same time he believes that the direction of modern social development leads toward a socialist organization of economic life. Instead of opposing this trend, we should meet the challenge to direct it into channels which will make for a peaceful transition and limit the dangers of turbulence and the outbreak of violence. Therefore Tönnies considered it important to implement the idea of *economic democracy*. Therefore he advocated and actively supported the workers' cooperative movement in Germany, as well as in Scandinavian countries, Switzerland, and Austria. Therefore he was in sympathy with plans for land reform and for the spread of adult and particularly workers' education, as a way to prepare technical employees and labor groups for the tasks they face in a changing economic order. He believed that a society which is ready to meet these challenges will have no reason to fear the trend toward socialist planning and he shared Friedrich Albert Lange's hope: "In the socialist movement we ought not to see a danger but the beginning of the rescue from a great danger."[21]

Though Tönnies firmly rejected the idea of a sudden and revolutionary change of the existing social system, he clearly recognized the institution of private ownership as a *historical* one. The legal and social order based upon private ownership, he believed, had contributed largely to the enormous growth of technological progress and economic wealth which many countries enjoyed during recent centuries. Yet, on the strength of his insight into the *historical* character of private ownership, he challenged its unqualified defence by those who regard it as "natural and necessary and therefore as sacred and inviolable."[22]

While the views of Tönnies already listed reveal his closeness to the Marxian position, we believe that the strongest likeness between the two writers lies in their treatment of the structure of modern society. The social framework of modern industrialized nations described by Marx is in many ways the archetype of Tönnies' *Gesellschaft*. This fact has often been overlooked because of the narrow interpretation generally given Marx's concept "capitalist society." This term, it is true, is used by Marx in a polemical sense, to express his condemnation of a social system with inherent exploitation and injustices. But he also uses it to describe the structure of a social order in which the strong communal organization of previous societies—for example, of tribal communities or medieval towns—no longer exists. In such societies individuals have become so separated and isolated that they establish contact only when they can use each other as means to *particular* ends: bonds between human beings are supplanted by useful associations, not of whole persons, but of particularized individuals.

Marx described these trends toward social atomization especially, though not exclusively, in his early writings— *On the Jewish Question, The Holy Family, The German Ideology, Introduction to a Critique of Hegel's Philosophy*

81

*of Law, Economic-Philosophical Manuscripts, Oekono
mische Studien, The Communist Manifesto,* and so on
We select some statements from the *Economic-Philo
sophical Manuscripts* and the *Oekonomische Studien.*
In these passages his thinking centers around Adam
Smith's theory that human society is to be regarded as
trading company and each one of its members as
merchant. Although he rejects the universal validity o
Smith's view, he finds it a revealing description of con
temporary industrial society. Marx calls this a caricatur
of true human community, since man has become s
isolated that his separateness from other men is accepted
as his natural form of existence and the human bond
which is the essence of mankind appears to be non
essential. In this situation "the social tie which I have t
you . . . is a mere semblance . . . our mutual supplement
ing is likewise a mere semblance." As Marx puts th
matter in another work of this period, the reality is
state in which man considers his fellow man as a means
degrades himself to a means, and so becomes a plaything o
alien forces.[24]

It is hard for us, according to Marx, to perceive thi
real condition, because it lies hidden behind the veil o
appearance and ideological construction. A gulf separate
our public existence from our personal existence, our role
as *citizens* from our roles as *private members of society*
There is a pronounced contrast between the heaven o
political doctrines and constitutional law, on the on
hand, and the earthly reality of the society in which w
live and act as private individuals and carry on our dail
occupations, on the other hand. The former expresses th

community of man; whereas the latter is indifferent to the relation of man to man and is based on fragmentary relationships, such as those established between landowner and tenant-farmer, capitalist and workman. Thus capitalist society does not embody *Gemeinschaft* but a state of separateness and discord, of unrestricted egotism, from which the *bellum omnium contra omnes* emerges.[25]

We have selected only a few of the numerous statements by Marx which show that, like Tönnies after him, he envisaged contemporary man as living in a society without human community, in a world in which he is barred from human fulfilment. This is the plight of "the dehumanized human being," of the alienated man, which was Marx's deepest concern and which became the central theme even of those of his writings which on the surface seem to deal exclusively with problems of economic history or economic theory. Thus it has been correctly stated (by a recent author who is deeply opposed to Marxian thinking) that Marx interpreted the history of his time, and in a broader sense, the history of capitalism, as the history of the alienation of man.[26]

Marx was not the first to present the idea of alienation. Since his early years his thinking had been gripped by Hegel's concept that separation and estrangement are at the heart of every form of reality. Even his angry opposition to *The Phenomenology of the Mind*, in which Hegel had developed this view, did not blind Marx to the "greatness" of its central thought. He was particularly moved by the idea that estrangement is a phase of the dialectical process, and that by experiencing and revolting against it man creates his own self and thus fulfills himself

83

as man. Yet Marx parted ways with Hegel. He was not primarily concerned with alienation as a universal principle but focused on its role in the contemporary period. In contrast with Hegel, he did not see his own age as one in which estrangement had given place to reconciliation and tranquility, and in which mankind, after arriving at a state of inner peace with itself, had at last come into its own. He saw instead forces of conflict and unrest, opposing trends tending to push beyond themselves and to drive the present process of history to transcend itself. Furthermore, Marx opposed Hegel's tendency to envisage alienation as "Spirit estranged from itself," as an event within the realm of mind. In this regard his orientation had much in common with that of Kierkegaard, his contemporary, who in turning against Hegel's system insisted that pure thought is a recent invention, a "lunatic postulate." In a similar vein Marx ridiculed all attempts at hypostatizing pure thought and especially what he understood to be the Hegelian view that "my real human existence [is] my philosophical existence."[27] His concern was not with alienation as a process within an abstract conceptual system but with the actual and concrete conditions of life which, according to him, produce man's alienation.

What are the forces that shape this real existence of modern man? To understand Marx's answer to this question, we have to recall his stress on Adam Smith's statement that society is a trading company and that everyone of its members is a merchant. Applying this concept not to society as such, but to its present stage of development, Marx describes the existence of contemporary man as largely shaped by the rise and dominant influence of commodity exchange.[28]

Marx considered the commodity to be the most elementary form of modern wealth and gave it a central position in his analysis of the economic and social features of capitalism. Both *Capital* and *A Contribution to the Critique of Political Economy* open with chapters which are entitled "Commodities." We cannot present in detail Marx's theory of the commodity but can only stress its main point. Marx considers the essence of the commodity the separation of use value from exchange value. No article, it is true, can become a commodity without having use value, that is, without having specific properties which make it fit to serve some consumer's needs. Although this use value is the *prerequisite* for the object's conversion into a commodity, *qua commodity* the object has only exchange value, and does "not contain as much as an atom of use-value."[29]

Marx's description of commodity production as the basis of the economic life of modern society has met with many objections. The most frequent criticism states that exchange of economic goods has been known in previous forms of society and did not start with the rise of capitalism. The argument is certainly correct to the extent that trade preceded the development of capitalist institutions, a fact which Marx not only noted but emphasized. A distinction must be made, however, between societies in which the exchange of goods is a more or less sporadic phenomenon and societies which are primarily geared to the production and sale of commodities. The difference is more than one of degree: it takes on a qualitative significance. Once commodity production has become the universal mode, all of man's economic activities and processes will center around it. Its main feature, exchange value, will reach out beyond the merely economic realm and penetrate the whole of human existence.[30]

This trend, Marx believes, has triumphed in the present age. Exchange value has long ceased to be a merely economic category: it has become the supreme value, the molding force of our lives. It exerts such a strong power over our minds that it comes between us and the world which surrounds us, making it impossible for us to be directly related to persons and things. Marx describes how the rule of the commodity has brought us to feel ourselves always as potential sellers or buyers, and how owning has become our strongest link with the world. "Private property has made us so stupid and one-sided that an object is *ours* only if we own it. . . . The sense of owning which represents the alienation of all the physical, intellectual and spiritual senses *has taken the place of all these senses.*" Marx insists that the individual who is reduced to such a "state of absolute poverty," to a mere fragment of a human being, has become unable to approach the world in inner freedom and therefore cannot experience its fullness and richness. The person who faces the world with the acquisitive spirit, with the one-sidedness emanating from focusing on exchange value, will see that the objects tend to recoil, fending him off from true possession. As an example Marx mentions the dealer in precious stones who can see only their commercial value but not their exquisite quality and beauty. He finds such an individual no better off than the poverty-stricken man who, absorbed in his misery, is incapable of responding to a scene of great beauty. It has been said that unshared wealth is the worst kind of poverty. In a similar vein Marx asserts: "We are

xcluded from *true* property because our *property* ex-
ludes the other man."[31]

It is easy to see here the parallel between Marx's
nalysis of commodity production and Tönnies' theory
f *Gesellschaft*. Both thinkers come to recognize the
eparation between man and man as the basic characteristic
f modern society. Marx finds that two relationships in
articular are dominated by the trend toward separation:
hat between the seller and the purchaser of a commodity;
nd that between employer and workman. We turn first
o his description of the ways in which seller and buyer
ssociate with each other.

It has often been said that capitalism has made tremendous strides toward the fulfilment of human needs.
Marx would have been the last to deny this assertion.
Even when he did not present his ideas with the calmness
f the scholar but with the stirring passion of the revolu-
ionary, he emphasized the great contribution of the
resent economic system. It has created, he says in *The
Communist Manifesto*, "more massive and more colossal
roductive forces than have all preceding generations
ogether."And he ends his description of the achievements
f the bourgeoisie with the question: "What earlier cen-
ury had even a presentiment that such productive forces
lumbered in the lap of social labour?" He cautions us,
however, against a false inference. To state that the life
f mankind would not have reached its present stage of
evelopment without commodity production is not the
ame as to assert that the fulfilment of human needs is
he goal of commodity production. Marx makes his point
y reminding us of the truism that the producers and

sellers of commodities, in spite of establishing contacts with numerous individuals and providing for their wants, have no real human bonds with them. They are exclusively concerned with the *equivalent* for the commodity they furnish. What gives your need for my article value, worth and importance for me is solely the article which you have to offer in exchange for mine. Your need and the portion of your property that you will give are thus synonymous and of equal worth for me. Your bidding only has meaning or result as it has meaning or result in relation to me. As a mere person without goods your demand will remain an unsatisfied aspiration for you, a baseless fancy for me. Thus as a human being you stand in no relationship to my object since I myself have no human relationship to it.[32]

All the many efforts to develop personalized salesmanship, to inject the so-called human touch into the dealings which lead up to the sale of commodities, serve only to make evident the fact that the relationship between sellers and buyers is one of means and ends. Commodity production is described by Marx as building up an elaborate system of catering to the consumer's wants while remaining truly unrelated to human need. Important as these wants are for the functioning of the economic system, the commodity producer sees them only as *objects*, as data on which to base his calculations and activities, as means without which he could not pursue *his* end. As Marx says, to the commodity producer any real or potential want appears as a weakness which can be used to draw the fly to the flypaper. To him every distress offers an opportunity to go over to his neighbor and to tell him

88

nder the semblance of cordiality: Friend, I will give ou whatever you long for; but remember there is one ondition, that you will have to pledge yourself to me in ndelible ink.[33]

The commodity seller who considers human needs a neans to accomplish *his* ends will often not be satisfied vith providing for existing wants. To increase them and o arouse new ones he will use skilful, though not always crupulous, devices. They are described by Marx in ungent words which have not lost their actuality and till apply today to efforts to make even children and dolescents victims of the traffic in narcotics and other timulants. He refers especially to the techniques used y the callous salesman to arouse a craving for morbid nd perverse pleasures in order stealthily to get hold of he silver and to entice the gold from his "neighbor" in pite of avowed Christian love for him.[34]

Even deeper than the split between seller and con- umer is the separation between commodity producer nd workman. The relationship between them forms a vorld which has been described succinctly in *Capital*.)ver its threshold, Marx says, is written: " 'No admittance xcept on business.' . . . The only force that brings them ogether and puts them in relation with each other, is the elfishness, the gain and the private interest of each. Each ooks to himself only, and no one troubles himself about he rest. . . ." Thus the association between employer nd laborer is dominated by a basic indifference to human eings, by an attitude which considers man as nothing nd the product as everything.[35]

This depersonalization has a deep impact on the

character of the work process. It converts the workman, in Marx's words, "into a cripple, a monster, by forcing him to develop [some] highly specialized dexterity at the cost of a world of productive impulses and faculties. . . . Not merely are the various partial operations allotted to different individuals; but the individual himself is split up, is transformed into the automatic motor of some partial operation."[36] Whereas in previous stages of economic development "the workman makes use of a tool, in the factory the machine makes use of him. There the movements of the instrument of labor proceed from him, here it is the movements of the machine that he must follow. In manufacture [as Marx calls the first stage of capitalist economy] the workmen are parts of a living mechanism. In the factory we have a lifeless mechanism independent of the workman, who becomes its mere living appendage." "Factory work," Marx states, "confiscates every atom of freedom, both in bodily and intellectual activity." To emphasize this point Marx quotes A. Ferguson, the contemporary of Adam Smith, who exclaimed, in describing modern economic life: "We make a nation of Helots, and have no free citizens."[37]

This loss of freedom—not, as has often been asserted, the inequality of salaries or the laborer's low income—is Marx's deepest concern. For him the essence of human work is freedom. "Of course," he says in the *Economic-Philosophical Manuscripts,* "the animal also produces. He builds a nest, builds a shelter for himself, as for example do the bees, beavers, ants. But the animal produces only what is immediately necessary for himself and for his young. . . . The animal produces only under the domination of immediate physical needs, while man produces even when he is free from physical needs, and produces freely for the first time when free from these needs."[38]

The character of work, however, has changed with the rise of the modern factory. Marx states that now the worker "does not fulfill himself in his work but denies himself. . . . He therefore only feels at home with himself away from work while in work he feels estranged from himself. His work is not voluntary but imposed, *forced labor*. It is . . . not the satisfaction of a need but only a *means* to satisfy needs extraneous to it. Its alienated character is clearly shown by the fact that, as soon as there is no physical or other compulsion, it is avoided like a plague. . . . Man (the worker) feels himself freely active in his animal functions such as eating, drinking, procreating . . . while in his human functions he feels ever more like an animal. The animal becomes the human and the human the animal."[39]

Although Marx emphasizes the dangers of alienated labor and its threat to human freedom he is far from noting only the negative and destructive aspects of alienation. As we have said before, he shares with Hegel the conviction that mankind comes into its own by going through the pains of estrangement and the struggle to overcome it. This is, according to Marx, what gives the work process its true meaning. Man projects his energies into the outside world, his life sinks into the product, it becomes "objectified," that is, materialized, in an object which appears to have an existence of its own. The gap which thus arises between the product and the forces which have created it is not necessarily a lasting one. It is closed when the product no longer remains outside of life but becomes reintegrated into it.

To illustrate this point, let us take an example from outside the realm of economics. Consider the artist who goes through a phase of alienation when he tries to express and to articulate an image. It is initially so identified and intertwined with him that he must endure pain and struggle to release it and give it a life of its own. Such a separation is necessary, however, to free the idea from the obscurity it has while it still dwells in the artist's soul. The severance becomes even more poignant when the artist, in the process of his creation, finds himself subject to laws which do not come from within but which are imposed on him from the outside, for example by the nature of the material and the tools with which he has to work or by the rules he has to follow. Yet out of this alienation a work of art may be born which is animated by the life the artist has breathed into it. In this moment he finds that his production is no longer severed from him but is taken back into his life, enriching and kindling it.

We have dwelt on the artist's experience because it sheds light on the nature of the work process as such alienation can lead toward reintegration in the realm of economic production too. It will do so, for example, when production is not an end in itself but is primarily geared to human needs, when man utilizes what he produces in the act of consumption or in the course of implementing further production. In both cases alienation, with all the suffering which it engenders, has not been in vain. By going through it and struggling to overcome it, man has succeeded in reaching a fuller life and taken one step more toward coming into his own.

It would be erroneous to conclude from this presentation that there is an easy or automatic transition from alienation to self-realization. Especially in present-day society, man finds it impossible to return from his condition of alienation to an integration with his world and with himself. To expose this condition and to reveal its causes was one of the major concerns of Marx's critique of capitalism. As we shall see later, he did not consider the alienation of man to be limited to capitalist society. He did believe, however, that in a system based on capitalist commodity production man's efforts to struggle against his alienation and to become reintegrated are most likely to be thwarted and doomed to fail.

In capitalist society the tendency to isolate exchange value from inherent qualities shapes our relation, not only to things, but also to human activities. Marx saw this development reaching its culmination in the realm of man's work, an insight which led to his central thesis that in present-day society man's labor power has become a commodity. He found it revealing that the classical school of political economy, in his view a true reflection of the existing economic structure, treated labor as merely one of the components of production, figuring in the capitalist's calculation along with other production costs, such as raw material, machinery, equipment, buildings, etc. Once labor has taken on the character of a commodity, work loses its human meaning. The product—likewise a commodity and subject to the law of the market—remains outside of the laborer's life. "The workman," Marx says, "sinks his life into the object; but then it does not any longer belong to him but to the object. . . . What the product of his work is, he is not." "The result of the laborer's externalization in his product is not only that his work becomes an object . . . but that the life with which he endowed this object faces him as something alien and hostile." Where this condition prevails work loses its true meaning of enabling man to realize himself. It is not any longer a medium for expressing and ful-filling one's *life* but is only a device for securing one's *livelihood*.[40] Even when this objective is achieved and a high price is attained for the sale of the commodity, labor-power, this price remains a surrogate, an "Ersatz." It can never take the place of the satisfaction experienced by man when he can find his own self in the products which he has created.

Labor can function as a commodity only when man's manual skills, his intellectual abilities and creative capaci-ties—in a word, the human qualities on which work is based—become detached from his person. They must be treated in the same way as capital, as a fund which through good management and investment will yield value. The worker must exist as capital in order to exist as a worker. To explain the full impact of this condition Marx adds: The worker can exist as capital only as long as capital exists to use him. The existence of capital is his existence; it shapes the content of his life, though remaining in-different to it.[41] The workman who is subject to this fate can hardly be anything else but a commodity in human form, an individual not belonging to himself but alien-ated from himself.

Marx's thesis that the workman's labor power has become a commodity has aroused severe criticism and is often considered as clearly outrageous. It is not hard to understand the intensity of this protest. Societies, like individuals, tend to cling to illusions about the forces which shape their lives. The reality lying beneath these illusions cannot be unveiled without pain.

Those who oppose the view that labor today is treated as a commodity can refer to the solemn language of the law. In Section 6 of the Clayton Act (1914), Congress enacted "That the labor of a human being is not a commodity or article of commerce." It seems to us, however, that this language does not describe an existing condition but formulates a desirable goal. This is confirmed by the wording in the Versailles Treaty, which in article 427 insisted that "labour should not be regarded merely as a commodity or article of commerce." Obviously this formulation is not meant to portray a factual situation but to establish an objective toward which our efforts should be directed.[42]

If we turn from legal terminology to everyday language, we find many expressions which reveal the conditions shaping the position of labor. It is not just by chance that we talk of a labor market, of labor supply, and of demand for labor, of labor import, labor surplus, and so on. All these terms would be meaningless if labor were not a commodity.

This characterization of labor is not confined to the language used in everyday life and in newspaper articles. The classical school of economics never concealed its tendency to treat labor as a commodity. Contemporary economists have usually viewed labor in the same way. In the standard work *Grundriss der Sozialökonomik*, which includes contributions by the leading scholars in the field of economics and sociology—such as Max Weber, Friedrich von Wieser, Joseph Schumpeter, and Werner Sombart—we read the following statement in the section on labor economics: "From the point of view of economics the workman faces the entrepreneur as the seller of his labor power." A more recent American book, *Labor Problems* by Professor W. V. Owen, asserts: "The treatment of labor as a commodity by employers is inherent in the capitalistic system which is founded on exchange carried on through the mechanism of price."[43]

There are many among Marx's critics who concede that the laborer's work has been turned into a commodity and that his life has become alienated. Deplorable as this fact may be, they argue, we should be careful not to exaggerate its impact; the laborers after all represent only one segment of an industrialized society. Therefore we should not overlook the importance of the various other groups which perform work operations of an entirely different nature. Marx himself—the argument goes on—has given the most vivid description of the contrast in the living conditions of the bourgeoisie and the working class. We agree of course with the statement that Marx emphasizes the great disparity in the situations of the opposing classes of contemporary society. It must be pointed out, however, that his analysis of this difference was remote from the simplification which both friends and foes of his concepts are inclined to impute to his thinking. It would be thoroughly incorrect to state that in Marx's opinion only the proletarians are the victims of tendencies which lead to man's alienation. "The possessing class and the class of the proletariat represent the same human self-estrangement," he affirms in an early work. This statement will hardly surprise us when we remember that he considers the commodity structure a *universal* phenomenon, which has a dominant influence on the whole of capitalist society, on the lives of both the workmen *and* the capitalists, and on the lives of all the other groups in society as well.[44]

This view will appear to many readers as a sweeping generalization. They will maintain that writers and artists, ministers and teachers, and members of other professions perform work which is essentially creative and in no way subjected to the forces of alienation which dominate the workman's job. This notion that the intellectual fulfills a very specific and distinctive function is widely spread. It is emphasized in many studies dealing with the sociology of knowledge, notably in Karl Mannheim's *Ideology and Utopia*, a work which has deeply affected the thinking of the generation between the two world wars.

One of the main concerns of Mannheim's book is to find the answer to the disturbing problem arising from inquiries into the relationship between mind and society. If our thoughts and even our modes of thinking are shaped by our specific social position, if each one of the segments of society—workers, industrialists, financiers, farmers, rural aristocracy and tenant farmers—looks at the same reality in different and often conflicting ways, how then can we still believe in a universal truth binding for all the strata of society? Mannheim saw the task of unifying the partial and limited views held by the various classes and he believed that such a synthesis could be achieved by persons who were not linked to particular groups and not drawn into their struggles. He had in mind the intelligentsia, the socially unattached intellectuals, whose aloofness would enable them to meet the challenge of integrating the one-sided and conflicting insights of the different components of society. He hoped that through the contribution of the intellectual, society would attain a more comprehensive grasp of reality, a more objective understanding of the truth.

We are well aware of the contribution which Mannheim has made to the work of contemporary sociology; but we cannot overlook the illusion which his optimistic faith in the role of the intellectual reflects, and which the events of the quarter century following the publication of *Ideology and Utopia* have so relentlessly destroyed. We have only to remember the actions of the German research scientists and physicians in the Nazi concentration camps, or to remark the capitulation of numerous American writers and university teachers before the present tendencies toward conformity, and we shall realize the fancifulness of Mannheim's thesis that it is the intelligentsia as a class to whom our age owes its understanding of objective truth. How can we explain that a scholar of Karl Mannheim's stature, who has done so much to dispel the illusions dominating the thinking of individuals and social groups, could maintain such an unrealistic view of the role of the intellectuals? One of the main reasons, we believe, has been his unwillingness to recognize the painful fact that in our society the work of the intellectual has become a commodity. We can well understand the reluctance of Mannheim and of many others to recognize this development. Its impact is disturbing even for Marx. Although he takes it for granted that the commodity structure rules over all realms of modern life, he finds it hard to prevent a feeling of despair from intruding upon the detachment of his analysis when he considers the tendency of the age to turn the creations of the mind into articles of commerce. In an early essay on the freedom of the press he expresses his indignation with any author who is primarily concerned with the market value of his writings. He asks: "Is the press true to itself, does it act in accordance with the nobility of its calling, is the press free when it debases itself to a commercial function?" This is how Marx answers his question: "It is true that the writer must make a living in order to exist and to write, but he ought not to exist and to write in order to make a living. A true writer in no way regards his works as a *means*. His works are ends in themselves. So little are they a means for him or others that when necessary, the writer sacrifices *his* existence to theirs. . . . Freedom of the press consists above all in its not being a business."[45]

Although this concern about the debasement of the role of the writer was expressed almost one hundred and twenty years ago, it does not seem to lack actuality today. In the last decade we have seen many an author who, in the face of political pressures, yielded to fear of being considered a dissenter and chose to follow a recognized and safe pattern of thinking. This political conformity, sometimes camouflaged by a tendency to withdraw from politics, to retreat from the public and to dwell on the private, is only one expression of the writer's readiness to consider his work more as a trade than as a calling. Another can be seen in the attempts of many writers to develop techniques designed to appeal to the literary market. A recent editorial in the *Saturday Review,* entitled "Fear as a Weapon," tries to find the reason for the present spread of fear, and gives this answer: "The American press is to some extent responsible. Bad news sells more papers than good news. The columnist must deliver his daily or weekly shocks. . . ." This statement seems to apply to many authors of short stories and novels who are no less preoccupied with the question: What sells?[46]

Perhaps the most serious impact of the writer's business orientation is that it leads him to encounter life from a literary point of view. He seems to become unable to look at his experiences as meaningful in themselves and he is haunted by a desire to consider even the most private and personal of them as material for literary use. Sometimes this may have a humorous aspect, as has been pointed out by Arthur Schnitzler in his play *Literatur.* An author and his friend, who is also a writer, decide to break off their romance. Each finds out that the other has written a novel centering around their affair. Both are dismayed when they discover that each of their books includes the complete collection of the love correspondence which had been exchanged between them. An angry dispute reveals that the lady had written a draft for every one of her letters and that she had collected all of these drafts for later literary use. Her friend had made a copy of each of his passionate notes and saved the duplicates with the same purpose in mind.[47]

When the writer becomes indiscreet about his own life it is not surprising that he displays an even greater disregard for the privacy of others. Romano Guardini, the Catholic philosopher, has described this tendency and illustrated it by the following example. The German magazine *Die Zeit* reported in its edition of September 6, 1951, that a radio script writer secretly dropped a microphone from his apartment to the open bedroom window of an elderly couple living on a lower floor. The very personal conversation which took place was broadcast in a performance presenting so-called "snapshots." It is true that the Nordwestdeutscher Rundfunk, the broadcasting company which produced this indiscreet program, had some doubts with regard to it. But the hesitations, which were based on legal rather than ethical considerations, were dropped when the ingenious author gave evidence that the persons whose conversations had been overheard and whose intimate experiences had been taped as documentary illustrations had consented in writing to their being made public on the radio. The reporter who wrote about the incident in *Die Zeit* saw the most discouraging aspect of it in the fact that the public accepted the "joke" without any sign of protest or indignation.[48]

We add another illustration, which we take from William Faulkner's interesting though disheartening article "On Privacy; the American Dream: What happened to it?" Faulkner argues that the attack on individual privacy is bad taste that "has been converted into a marketable . . . commodity by the merchandizing federations which at the same simultaneous time create the market . . . and the product to serve it." He recounts his own victimization by a magazine writer who, in spite of Faulkner's pleading, could not be deterred from writing an article about his private life. He describes how he found himself caught in a situation of complete helplessness, how he saw himself doomed regardless of what step he took, whereas the publisher was likely to gain no matter what happened. "And even if there had been grounds for recourse, the matter would still have remained on the black side of the ledger since the publisher could charge the judgement and costs to operating loss and the increased sales from the publicity to capital investment." We have referred to Faulkner's article because it shows how an author whose thinking has little in common with Marx's became aware through his own experience that he was not respected as a writer. In Faulkner's own words, he was treated "as a commodity: merchandise: to be sold, to increase circulation, to make a little money." He came to see this business orientation which dominates so much modern writing as "destroying the last vestige of privacy without which man cannot be an individual."[49]

The tendencies which we have described are not confined to the writer: they also have a strong impact on the work of the teacher, the lawyer, the minister and the physician. Idealists in these professions often experience conflicts resulting from the fact that society tends to turn their services into products. Comparing business and the professions, A. T. Hadley, at one time president of Yale University, wrote in 1923: "The line between the two is somewhat ill-defined and I am afraid the tendency in recent years has been to shift in the wrong direction— to commercialize our medicine and our law and our

science, rather than to professionalize our business."[50]
Facts which support Hadley's thesis are numerous, and
will come easily to the reader's mind. We don't find it
necessary to present examples, since the alienation of the
work of the professional man is one of the major themes
of C. Wright Mills's well known book *White Collar* and
since we refer to some aspects of this subject in the second
part of the following chapter.

CHAPTER FIVE

Retrospect and Outlook: Can
Alienation Be Overcome?

THE AWARENESS of man's alienation, the idea that—as the existential philosophers say—we are and remain strangers in this world, pervades the thinking of our period. The preceding chapters of this book have tried to show that the emphasis on this idea reflects two closely related trends which shape the character of modern society: the transition from *Gemeinschaft* to *Gesellschaft*, as seen by Ferdinand Tönnies, and the growing predominance of commodity production, as described by Marx. In the following pages we want, first, to examine two main objections to this interpretation, and then to consider the question: Can alienation be overcome?

The first criticism is that the importance of technology is overlooked. Those who express this opinion claim that only by focusing on the relationship between man and machine will we be able to understand the forces which cause alienation. This view dominates a vast literature. Romano Guardini has summed it up in the example to which we have already referred. "When one person strikes down another with the help of a weapon, he is able to experience his action in an immediate way. This will be quite different when he pushes a button from an airplane at great height, and hundreds of thousands of people below die. He has been fully cognizant of his action and able to bring it about, but he cannot feel it as immediate experience."[1]

Like Romano Guardini, Gunther Anders has emphasized the indirectness of modern man's encounter with reality. In his article "The World as Phantom and as Matrix" he describes how, as a result of radio and television, "the events come to us, not we to them." He shows that the world presented to us at home in our chairs is one which we look at and accept but which we do not make our own, so that, acting as eavesdroppers and Peeping Toms, we rule over a phantom world.[2]

Such statements as those of Guardini and Anders are valid in themselves, but often lead to false conclusions. Guardini's illustration, for example, can be erroneously used to show that the advancement of technological knowledge, which led to splitting the atom, is the *cause* of the tragedy of Hiroshima. The fallacy here becomes obvious when we realize that the condition of an event is not identical with its cause. Nuclear physics is the medium through which the destruction of war is carried out, is the *condition* of modern war. To say however that we have war because we have nuclear physics would mean to accept a technological determinism which implies that man can do nothing to avoid a global catastrophe.

Gunther Anders' description could also prompt a false inference. His observations on the low level of radio and television programs seem quite justified. The view presented in these pages is close to his, especially when he describes many radio and television programs as possessing "the characteristics of an assembly line product," of a home-delivered "commodity."[3] But much as we agree with his analysis, we find it necessary to add that while the tendencies in recreational life which he criticizes have been increased and immensely intensified by radio and television, they have not been initiated by them. Long before the advent of such programs, the "entertainment industry" had been dominated by the commodity structure. It had seen its role as providing the public, in exchange for an admission fee, with artificial excitement, with thrills, sensationalism, and slap-stick humor, and not with programs that would arouse people in a genuine way by making them face the real questions and conflicts of human life.

We have presented this critique of Guardini and Anders because their statements typify a widespread tendency to blame the machine and the rise of technology for too much. To illustrate, let us go back to an example given earlier, in our description of threats to privacy. Is it really the fault of the microphone when it is used by a shrewd reporter to broadcast what is going on in the bedroom of an elderly couple? Technology can be employed either for good or evil purposes. The lens of a camera can be used to catch the splashing serenity of a brook flowing through a valley or the majestic beauty at the zenith of a mountain. It can also be used to snap pictures of crime and accidents, which will increase the circulation of the magazines and newspapers, or to photograph obscene acts for portrayal on postcards which can be sold to the masses.

All of this points up what has often been said, that the machine is ethically indifferent and that the dormant forces of technology can be activated for good or evil. This frequently stated view has been presented in a very concise form by Bishop Gerald Ensley at the Ninth World Methodist Conference: "We must not forget," he declares, "that every gift of science can be used to further evil. . . . The chemistry that gives us the wonder drugs that liberate from pain can also supply narcotics which will enslave a man all the days of his life. . . . The plane that can rush food or antibiotics to a beleaguered city can also visit worse than black death upon it. Science gives us instruments of both good and evil without determining the quality of the ends for which they shall be employed."[4]

There is not much chance, we fear, that Bishop Ensley's argument will receive the careful examination it deserves. Many people are inclined to accept hastily the indictment of science and technological development, without realizing that technology is neutral in itself and does not determine the ends for which it is used. They are not prepared to recognize that its most lamentable results actually grow out of *our* aims and choices—specifically out of the values of a society whose members, as noted by Marx in a statement quoted above, have surrendered their whole being to the one sense of owning.

Our view that the values of society do not emanate from technology as such will undoubtedly be criticized. It will be said, for example, that technology, by making it so easy for us to manipulate our environment in an effortless way, produces a frame of mind which is entirely dominated by the passion for control and does not respond to any values but efficiency and success. In her interesting observations on "The American Standard of Living," Elizabeth Hoyt says: "We have worked ourselves up and set ourselves going, and we do not know how to stop. . . . It was once said of the typical American businessman that he puts his family in the car on Sunday and starts out for somewhere or nowhere as fast as he can go. When he gets home, 'he squints at the speedometer to see if he had a good time.' It is no accident that the current ideal of successful leisure is to 'go places.' "[5]

Such a climate—many people, and in particular many artists, contend—accounts for our leaning toward materialistic values and for the stifling of true creativity. This argument should not be dismissed lightly. The statement that technological advancement has enormously facilitated the achievement of our goals is certainly correct. It must be seen, however, that an account of the forces which have made the *attainment* of our values so much easier stops short at explaining *why we have chosen these values.*

Our thesis that the alienation experienced by man today results from economic and social trends of the modern age will be challenged with a further objection. It is wrong, many will say, to see human estrangement as a characteristic of a specific period and not to recognize that it is a phenomenon which has occurred in all ages of history. Those who hold this view like to point out that the creative person has always had to pay the price of loneliness, to experience the pain of estrangement. Sweeping arguments of this kind have in our view a very limited validity. History has witnessed (we agree) the suffering of imaginative and unique men who, not understood by their own age, have met with nothing but contempt and suspicion. But history has also witnessed the deep sense of belonging which inspired the genius of many creative individuals, whose bonds with their communities enabled them to sense the pulse and the needs of their age and to express in their works the thoughts and dreams of their less articulate fellow men. And even those among the creative men of the past who found themselves impelled to break away from their communities, from the accepted ways of thought, did not experience the kind of isolation which has become the fate of the atomized individual living in modern society. Their existence was tragic but it was not meaningless. They did not surrender their own selves; and in all their loneliness they did not go to pieces, as modern men do when they try to play roles which are alien to them.

The idea that man's alienation is not confined to the modern period but must be understood as a universal fate of human existence is widely accepted today. It is in line with one of the dominant trends in contemporary thought, which under Kierkegaard's influence has tended to turn away from the optimistic beliefs of the eighteenth and nineteenth centuries and is moving toward a deepened awareness of "the tragic sense of life." To those who follow this way of thinking, the alienation which modern man experiences in the relationship between man and man, and in the realm of work, appears as a manifestation of a very much more fundamental trend: his estrangement from God. The myth of man's fall, present in some form or other in all stages of history, reflects, according to this interpretation, man's awareness that he has lost his primordial union with the divine. "The essence of sin," Paul Tillich writes, "is disbelief, the state of estrangement from God, the flight from him, the rebellion against him. . . . Man is bound to sin in all parts of his being, because he is estranged from God in his personal center. . . . His intellectual power is as distorted and weakened as his moral power. . . . Intellectual endeavor can as little attain the ultimate truth as moral endeavor can attain the ultimate good. He who attempts it deepens the estrangement."[6]

Tillich's words make us aware that those who really wrestled with the idea of sin, men like Paul, Augustine, Luther, and later on Kierkegaard, did not look at it simply as an abstract concept, worthy of interesting theological and philosophical speculation. They sensed in it the frightful reality of man's alienation from God. But Tillich's statements are misunderstood, we believe, when they are used to prove that in all ages of history mankind has experienced the same kind and measure of alienation as today. Such an interpretation seems to us mistaken, because the specific idea of sin which Tillich emphasizes, alienation from God, is historically speaking only one of various concepts of sin and has often been overshadowed by less tormenting views. Tillich himself refers to the tendency of many preachers and even theologians to identify sin with moral wrong-doing, to use the word primarily in the plural, and to speak of sins as indulgences in temporal pleasures forbidden by religion, tradition, or convention—such as drinking, dancing, cursing, gambling, and adultery.[7]

Moreover, it is important to remember that the great religious leaders who saw man's alienation from God as the essence of sin had in many cases only a limited impact on the thinking of their period. Ernst Troeltsch, the outstanding theologian and historian, has shown in a famous study that St. Augustine, for example, influenced the doctrine of the medieval church to a far lesser extent than has been generally assumed. He points out that the outlook of the Middle Ages was largely unaffected by the pessimistic view of man as a rejected creature, forever estranged from the Lord.[8]

For all these reasons we find it hard to agree with those who use Tillich's idea of sin to prove that estrangement is a universal human condition and that the alienation experienced by the individual today is man's eternal fate. In opposing this view we do not contend, however, that human lives have become alienated *only* since the rise of the modern age, specifically since the growth of commodity production and the transition from *Gemeinschaft* to *Gesellschaft*. Trends toward alienation were at work in previous societies too. Recognition of this fact, however, can easily lead to an abstract and unhistorical view of alienation. To say that forces alienating human lives have influenced all stages of man's development leaves important questions unanswered. (It is no more meaningful than to assert that there has always been anti-Semitism— a proposition which, even if true, would be inadequate to give a real understanding of the causes and significance of the persecution of the Jews in Nazi Germany.) Such a statement does not tell us anything about the varying intensity of these forces in different periods of history or about the extent of their impact on the diverse segments of society.

Let us illustrate this point by referring to the widely held opinion that during the Middle Ages most people were subject to such a large measure of drudgery and to such wretched working conditions that they were barred from any kind of self-realization. The medieval town was certainly not the idyllic world portrayed by its romantic admirers. There were petty rivalries between guilds. Many of them stipulated strict entrance requirements in their effort to become more exclusive and to establish mastership as a hereditary privilege.[9] They were anxious to expand the power of the master craftsmen at the expense of the rights of journeymen and apprentices. Yet in spite of the conflicts and tensions to which the craftsman in the medieval town was exposed, on the whole he found his work related to his life and it meant more to him than just a means to making a living. He was part of a recognized group. Although in the last centuries of the Middle Ages it was made hard for him to improve his status within the guild, he did not experience the isolation from his fellow man which has become the fate of the individual living in the atomized society of today.

It is true, of course, that a large part of the population was more directly affected by the feudal structure of medieval society than were the townspeople. The serfs lived in extremely precarious and miserable conditions and were often treated in a cruel and inhuman way. Their obligations toward their masters were burdensome, and the obedience required of them made it impossible for them to make their own decisions. We should be careful,

113

however, not to let our indignation about these conditions interfere with our historical understanding of the characteristic traits of medieval serfdom. The tendency to identify feudal serfdom with slavery is mistaken, as has been shown by Marx and by more recent authors. The eminent French historian, Marc Bloch, has emphasized at the end of the first volume of his monumental work *La Société Féodale,* that the serfs' conditions did not at all represent a mitigated version of ancient slavery or of the Roman colonate. He points out that the serf as a tenant had the same duties and rights as anybody else: his possession was not more precarious; the proceeds from his work, once his debts were paid and his services rendered, were his own. Bloch also makes the point, stressed even more strongly by George C. Homans, that between lord and peasant there existed, not only the cold relationship which holds between creditor and debtor, but also direct human bonds. It may be questioned whether the relations between the serfs and their masters were as reciprocal, and whether as strong a solidarity existed between them, as Bloch and especially Homans contend. But even if this point has been overemphasized by these authors, we can state that the condition of the serfs, and even more of the journeymen, makes it appear doubtful whether the concept of alienation applies to the same extent to the Middle Ages as to the modern period.[10]

Furthermore it must be said that in the course of history alienation has undergone significant qualitative changes, that its meaning today is quite different from what it was in previous eras. In the present stage of history man has means of self-realization at his command which were unknown to him in former periods. The immense advance of science and technology has helped him to understand the forces of nature to such a degree that he is not any longer at their mercy: he has become their master and has succeeded in subjecting them to *his* ends. With this tremendous progress toward the realization of the Promethean dream, a new image has arisen of man who shapes his life and is master of his destiny. Once this concept of the individual's sovereignty has been awakened in the minds of men, a new climate is prepared. The consciousness that man's yearning for self-realization is thwarted becomes a crushing experience which could not have existed in previous stages. In such a situation the alienation of man is not any longer accepted as an inevitable fate; more than ever before in history it is felt as a threat and at the same time as a challenge.[11]

Can alienation be overcome? Those who consider estrangement as inherent in human existence will of course deny that it can be conquered by man's action. For them it is best that the individual resign himself to his state of alienation, instead of pursuing the vain dream that it is up to him to change his condition.

Our own answer is quite different from this view. The awareness that man in all stages of history has undergone some form and degree of alienation, and that this will be his fate also in the future, does not take from him the obligation to struggle against those forms of alienation which he meets today. The knowledge that there always has been and always will be sickness is hardly a reason for medical science to abandon its fight against the forms of disease which now threaten us. The belief that mankind will ever succeed in freeing itself from alienation might be an unfounded hope. But in giving it up we should not ignore the challenge to come to grips with those forms of alienation which are predominant in our period.

To strive toward this aim does not mean to dream of the millenium. In order to illustrate this point, we refer to Marx's thinking on the conquest of alienation. Deeply committed to the struggle against the forces of commodity production, which in his view had brought about modern man's alienation, he did not fall a prey to the Chiliastic hope that in the society of the future mankind would find the answer to all its pains and conflicts, that it would reach the highest and last stage of human development. As a youth he had said: "Communism is the necessary form and the active principle of the immediate future, but communism is not itself the aim of human development or the final form of human society." Toward the end of his life he expressed this thought again. In the closing chapters of the third volume of *Capital* he asserted that even after the elimination of commodity production, *and no matter what form society takes,* man's life and work will always be dominated by forces which act upon his will from the outside and which interfere with his dream of self-realization, with his efforts freely to shape his life in nature and society. "In fact the realm of freedom does not commence until the point is passed where labor under the compulsion of necessity and of external utility is required. In the very nature of things it lies beyond the sphere of material production in the strict meaning of the term. Just as the savage must wrestle with nature, in order to satisfy his wants, in order to maintain his life and reproduce it, so civilized man has to do it, and he must do it *in all forms of society and under all possible modes of production.* With his development the realm of natural necessity expands, because his wants increase; but at the same time the forces of production increase, by which these wants are satisfied. Freedom in this field can consist only of the fact that socialized man, the associated producers, regulate their interchange with nature rationally, bring it under their common control, instead of being ruled by it as by some blind power; that they accomplish their task with the least expenditure of energy and under conditions most adequate to their human nature and most worthy of it. But it always remains a realm of necessity. Beyond it begins that development of human power which is its own end, the true realm of freedom, which, however, can flourish only upon that realm of necessity as its basis. The shortening of the working day is its fundamental prerequisite."[12]

Although Marx did not harbor the hope that fundamental economic and social changes would bring the millenium, he considered them *indispensable* to coping effectively with the forms of alienation prevailing in modern society. Tönnies' thinking proceeded in a similar direction. As we have pointed out, he saw no immediate way to check the trend toward estrangement between man and man engendered by *Gesellschaft.* For him the only glimmer of hope was that in a society arising in the distant future the characteristics of *Gemeinschaft* and *Gesellschaft* would be integrated. In his own time, he contended, all

117

that could be done was to contribute in an indirect way to this long-range development. This is why he favored (among other measures) the strengthening of producers' and consumers' cooperatives. He expected the spread of these organizations to be instrumental in re-establishing "use value" as the directing principle of economic life; and he hoped they would increasingly take the place of business enterprises working for profit on private capital investment.[13]

To-day most of those who seek to overcome alienation are unwilling to follow the approaches proposed by Marx or Tönnies. They consider alienation as a state of mind and believe that an inner change, a spiritual rebirth, will enable man to return from this condition. Many of them emphasize the need for a revived and deepened religious commitment, although not necessarily for a return to institutionalized religion. Others concentrate on efforts to reinterpret human knowledge. Inspired by men like Bergson, Husserl, Scheler, and Heidegger, they try to break away from the cult of natural science, which is focused almost exclusively on detached knowledge, and they grope for ways toward an encounter with reality which is based on participation. There are also those who believe that the minds of the young, at least, can be protected from the influence of alienating forces, and that therefore we should be concerned with the improvement of teaching methods. Some groups emphasize the need for the strengthening of neighborhood feeling and grass roots responsibility, or for a larger participation in the tasks of local government. Furthermore, many people influenced by the ideas of the "do-it-yourself" movement

expect that practical hobbies will induce man to familiar-
ize himself with tools and materials, and thus help him
to grow into a new closeness to the objects of his environment.

Efforts of the kind we have described are important,
because they reveal that many people today no longer
accept man's estrangement as an inevitable fate but are
reaching for ways of conquering it. Are the moves which
they suggest steps in the right direction? To answer this
question, let us look briefly at some of these attempts to
counteract the trend toward alienation and see what they
have accomplished so far.

The call for a return to religion seems to find a strong
response in these days; at least it looks this way if statistics
of church membership and attendance figures of religious
services are considered as valid criteria. It is quite possible
that beneath the new emphasis on the religious life there
is a more genuine seeking than mere numbers reveal.
But who would seriously assert that this growing concern
about religion has so far had any effect on man's daily
existence, on his business and professional life, on his relations to his fellow man and to his political community?

Moreover, it is hard to deny that the religious resur-
gence itself has fallen prey to the very forces of alienation
which it is allegedly destined to conquer. The advantages
of a return to religion are extolled with the help of advertising techniques which are not very different from those
successfully used in the sales promotion of commodities.
The tendency to make religion comfortable, against which
Kierkegaard protested, has become more and more predominant in the religious life of our day. Often it is

119

coupled with an attitude for which the object of faith or belief is not God, but rather the utility of faith or belief. In recent years many theologians have been troubled by this development, which has led many people to consider faith in God to be mainly a way to achieve personal happiness or peace of mind, a mere tool, as important for our spiritual health as technological gadgets may be for our physical welfare. In an article which deals primarily with religious services in suburban centers but which is also revealing about the place of religion in our modern civilization, Stanley Rowland Jr. has stated: "The main mood of many a suburban church on Sundays is that of a fashionable shopping center. . . . On weekdays one shops for food, on Saturdays one shops for recreation and on Sundays one shops for the Holy Ghost." Mr. Rowland's statement and his whole article seem to us significant because of his grasp of a situation in which religion too has become a commodity. Where this trend prevails, the inner structure of the religious congregation undergoes a significant change. It is no longer a *church,* a group united by spiritual bonds, but tends to become an *audience* to which the minister delivers his sermon in much the same way as a speaker addresses his *public.* As long as these conditions of contemporary religious life persist, as long as religion itself is invaded by forces which grow out of the dominance of the commodity structure, the return to religion, we believe, will be nothing but the return to the alienated forms of religion. It will hardly show the way man can conquer his estrangement.[14]

Can we find more promise in the development of contemporary philosophical thought? To answer this question, let us go back to the trends in the first decades of this century, as these were described at the beginning of this book. The thinking of many individuals and groups had been swayed by Husserl's insistence on a scrutiny of the principles of philosophical orientation, by his demand for a return to the object. Many found their own longing expressed in this challenge. Husserl's goal seemed to formulate the innermost need of the age: to bridge the gulf between subject and object; and, by overcoming this split, to conquer man's estrangement from his world and from himself. As time went by, however, many who had shared this belief in Husserl's work became disillusioned. They began to realize that he had failed in his struggle to lay a new foundation for the fulfilment of the philosophical task and that his own thinking had been seized by tendencies which perpetuated the cleavage between subject and object.

Some of Husserl's disciples, it is true, have been very much aware of this failure. Although accepting his method, they have tried to broaden it. By including man's existence in the scope of phenomenological inquiry, they have hoped to find a more promising way for philosophy to fulfill its role, that is, to heal the sickness of an alienated world. But so far there is little indication that the efforts of our contemporary existential philosophers have achieved their goal. The core of existential philosophy *expresses* man's alienation. It hardly shows—and according to many of its advocates does not even claim to show—a way out of the estrangement which has been inflicted upon man.

Heidegger in the first stage of his work has described man as he is swayed by the ways of the anonymous "they," instead of listening to his conscience, which calls him to be himself, to commit himself unconditionally to the law of his inner self. Following Heidegger, Sartre has stated that man, thrown into a world which has no road signs, cannot be told which way to go, which values he ought to choose. He has to choose his own person, and there is no guide-post along the road but the awareness that only total involvement counts. As much as this idea appeals to contemporary man, it does no more than reflect his desire to return from his alienated existence, from a condition in which he has become a mere object.

This must also be said about the second stage of Heidegger's work, in which he urges us to rethink the relationship between man and Being, to awaken from that numbness toward Being into which man has fallen since he started to fancy Being as one of his contrivances and subject to his autonomous manipulation. This obliviousness toward Being, inherent in the thinking of the crowd and in a technological orientation, is *the* danger which threatens man; it is deadlier than all the particular hazards he encounters, deadlier even than the bomb. The night into which we are plunged will only yield when we retreat, not only from the hustle of our frantic activities, but also from the alleged triumph of calculating thought, when the awareness that man is woven into Being and its fate makes us ready for the silence in which the soundless voice of Being speaks to us.[15]

Critics have emphasized the extreme polarity between the two stages in Heidegger's work. In the first he focuses on the voice of conscience, which calls man to full commitment, to resoluteness of decision and action. In the second he is concerned with the voice of Being, which can be heard by those who in a somewhat esoteric fashion have retreated from the outlook of the masses and the thinking of the technological age. But it seems to us that the two periods are linked together through the central theme of human estrangement. As much as Heidegger has done to make us aware of this problem, he has not shown us the way toward its solution. In no stage of his work has he gone beyond the formulation of a stirring but futile protest against man's alienation.

If religion and philosophy prove ineffective, will a solution be found in the reform of education? The hope is sometimes expressed that improved methods of teaching will prepare young people to resist alienating forces. The revolt against mere book knowledge, together with the influence of pragmatist thought on our educational philosophy, has led to the widely accepted demand for "learning by doing," for basing the learning process upon techniques to stimulate the student's self-activity. This approach is supposed to enable him to find out for himself, to establish that close relationship between himself and reality which is the most effective defence against the danger of alienation.

The progress in the development of sound educational philosophies and effective teaching methods has been considerable. These accomplishments, however, are no panacea. They have not resulted in warding off a crisis which affects the lives of a large number of young people. Often we are told that the alarming statistics about the low scholastic achievements of our youth are exaggerated and give too dark a picture. It is claimed that critical evaluation of these discouraging reports would show how much they are colored by the tendency of adults in all periods of history to idealize the past, to lament new ways of life and especially the behavior patterns of the rising generation. Implied in these arguments is the view that moralizing complaints about our depraved youngsters are thoughtless, that nothing is to be gained by such a condemnation. Even if we agreed with this opinion, we would find it necessary to add that on the other hand nothing is gained by ignoring the fact that large numbers of our younger generation are disturbed by a deep restlessness, and that this state of crisis continues unabated in spite of all our progress in educational theory and practice and in the field of child and youth psychology.

What accounts for the ineffectiveness of the educational approach? It would be somewhat consoling if we could blame the situation primarily on temporary factors, such as the inadequacy of finances for our school programs and the insufficiency of appropriate physical facilities for our schools. The classroom shortage, estimated early in 1957 at 159,000 according to the figures of the United States Office of Education; the number of excess students, which amounts to 2.3 millions out of a total 31.5 millions; the low level of teachers' salaries, forcing many of them to supplement their income by taking on additional jobs—these are difficulties which grow out of present-day conditions. As hard as these problems are and as remote as we are now from finding a satisfactory answer to them, there is hope that the efforts of civic-minded individuals and groups, together with responsible government agencies, might succeed in achieving their solution in some future day.[16]

It is harder to hold out this hope in regard to even more serious difficulties in our educational life. They arise, for example, when appointments of teachers and other decisions affecting the functioning of our schools do not grow out of a genuine concern for the children, but result from pressures and manipulations on the part of influential politicians. They arise when teachers, aware of the insecurity of their position, either surrender to the demand for conformity or become reluctant to deal with the issues of our age, discussion of which might reveal the teacher's own values, when they escape instead into that neutrality, often presented as objectivity, which reduces teaching to the imparting of merely "factual" but essentially uninspiring knowledge.

All these difficulties in meeting the challenge of education are underscored by a condition which is even more basic and disturbing. A few years ago Henry Locke Anderson Jr., a student graduating *magna cum laude* from Williams College, delivered an address at commencement exercises which was considered the best speech and earned him the Dewey prize. These are some of the things he had to say: "Our educations have lacked any real meaning. Not only have we been apathetic toward intellectual life, we have even fled from it, endlessly seeking diversion both in and out of the class room. . . . We are, most of us, not intellectually tolerant, we only are gullible; we are not sceptical, we are only suspicious; not sophisticated, only apathetic; not humble, only confused. . . . *Worst of all we are not at all enthusiastic, curious or even interested.* . . . We have had countless opportunities to quench whatever intellectual thirst we might have—an excellent faculty, a good library, a provocative curriculum—but having been led to these streams of knowledge, we have apparently been disinclined to drink therefrom."[17]

Those who are concerned about the condition described by Mr. Anderson are often inclined to put the blame on our schools. Many accuse our educational institutions, not only of failing to stimulate the student's curiosity, but even of stifling it. There seems to be some evidence, on the surface at least, to justify this criticism. The great emphasis on grades, for example, often leads to situations in which the student's inner motivation is overshadowed and even destroyed by his desire to secure high marks. As disturbing as we may find this trend, we should not forget the fact that it is not just a development within the educational field but a result of the pressures of a competitive society on the orientation and functioning of its schools.

There are other indications that education, far from creating new attitudes, primarily reflects and confirms the values and tendencies pervading the existing society. One of the basic goals of our period seems to be development of the adjusted man, who gets along with people and whose thinking does not differ from the generally accepted values and norms. Our schools are trying eagerly to imbue the students with this ideal. It also becomes the standard for the desirable instructor. Many teachers are today—as Arnold A. Rogow has pointed out in a recent article— "not so much educators as group leaders whose self-esteem is tuned solely to harmonious relations with the students, the principal and superintendent, the parents and the community at large."[18] Sometimes the student's apathy is attributed to the preoccupation of our educational institutions with training mere technicians. The kind of teaching which has become increasingly prevalent often provides the student with the mastery of specialized and frequently very useful skills; but it is a highly compartmentalized teaching, which focuses exclusively on partial and fragmentary aspects of the problem under study and denies the student a moving encounter with the wholeness of the phenomenon or issue he is trying to grasp. Many responsible individuals, inside and outside the educational profession, have become aware of this shortcoming in our teaching. Every year, about the beginning of June, in hundreds of solemn commencement speeches the members of the graduating classes are urged to remember that the most precious value of knowledge is not its capacity to increase our power over nature and to raise our position in society, but its human meaning, that is, its capacity to enable man to carry through his search for truth which makes him free. In addition to these addresses, thousands of articles are written lamenting the cult of success and urging our younger generation to pursue their studies without concern for external rewards.

So far all these appeals have not borne much fruit. They have remained ineffective largely because they ignore many influences operating in modern culture which have the effect of counteracting the rise of a new attitude toward knowledge. In our age the salaries and the social status which are attained in industry and in many technological occupations are much higher than those which are attained by artists, teachers, librarians, ministers, and social workers. We stress those elements of knowledge which are primarily factual and which, when successfully memorized, can help us to "strike it rich" and to achieve a triumph worth $64,000 on a television program. Accordingly, we can hardly expect young people to respond eagerly to lofty ideas about the inner meaning of knowledge and about the danger of debasing the noble cause of learning by subordinating it to monetary and prestige values. This situation is neither helped nor really understood by those who launch bitter attacks against the materialistic spirit of the present generation. It grows out of basic tendencies which for centuries have been at the core of our thinking. Modern man does not seek knowledge primarily to understand the mystery of being or to find answers to the questions awakened by the sense of wonder allegedly inherent in all human beings. He prefers the type of learning which enables him to achieve his goal of subjecting the world to his ends and increasing his power over both nature and his fellow men. The knowledge which serves this purpose best is the pragmatic, controlling knowledge described in Scheler's studies on the sociology of modern thought. The emphasis on this knowledge for control is a basic trend of modern civilization. It will be reversed neither by admonition nor by steps taken at present by some of our educational institutions and contemplated by others. For example, changes of the curriculum designed to increase the number of liberal arts courses would hardly be a corrective, since there is ample evidence that the Humanities are not a sanctuary at the threshold of which the described trend would stop. They too are deeply influenced by the predominance of pragmatic, controlling knowledge. Appointment of scholars trained in the tradition of classical studies as presidents of leading universities,[19] and programs of teaching and research which, with the help of so-called roving professors, would cut through the conventional boundaries separating the various university departments, are measures which some educators hope may help to temper the tendencies toward compartmentalization of present day teaching. Yet it seems very doubtful that steps of this kind will change the basic direction of modern knowledge.

We turn now to those forces within political life which many people expect will help to conquer the trend toward alienation. The hope is often expressed that a reawakening of the spirit pervading our institutions of local self-government would challenge the citizen to participate in the conduct of public affairs and would liberate him from his present state of aloofness. Those who voice this expectation frequently refer to the authority of Lord Bryce, who in his famous work *The American Commonwealth* described local self-government as "not merely beneficial, but indispensable," contending that "it stimulates the interest of people in the affairs of their neighborhood, sustains local political life, educates the citizen in his daily round of civic duty, teaches him that perpetual vigilance and the sacrifice of his own time and labor are the price that must be paid for individual liberty and collective prosperity."[20]

In recent times the development of many communities has proceeded in a direction which seems to justify the views expressed by Lord Bryce and his present-day admirers. The pronounced growth of suburban life has aroused hope for a rebirth of the forces of political and cultural decentralization, and with it of a more active participation by the individual in the concerns of his community. Lately, however, we have become aware that the hopes with which we have viewed these trends have been too high, that suburban developments, far from counteracting the tendencies which dominate the political and cultural life of modern society, implement and strengthen them.[21] The need for a more sober appraisal of suburban life is expressed in a number of articles and books, such as those by Spectorsky, Whyte, and Keats, which challenge some of our complacent notions. They are especially revealing with regard to the question of participation, which is our immediate concern. Whyte describes how the typical resident of the suburb has to plunge into a "hotbed of participation," how he belongs to numerous committees and groups, and how only by careful scheduling of his engagements can he be saved "from being expected at two different meetings at the same time."[22]

But in many cases it appears that joining all these hectic group and committee activities stems from the desire not to be considered an outsider and brings about an uncritical adaptation to the pressures and standards of the group. Whyte's book is full of examples which show that life in suburban communities engenders conformity, lack of privacy, and abandonment of individual values. Far from encouraging the kind of participation visualized by Lord Bryce, far from conquering human estrangement, it fosters that tendency to drift which, according to Heidegger, is the fate of all those who do not follow their own selves but think and act with the anonymous "they."

The relationship between the whole and its parts is far from being a merely philosophical problem. It has an important bearing on most scientific disciplines, including the social sciences. Concepts like "the whole of society" or "the structure of society" are often considered suspect and sterile; there are even some writers who want to abandon them altogether. Many social scientists feel that the development of reliable empirical research methods has been stifled by the focus on society as a whole. They point out that a stronger emphasis on detailed phenomena and on procedures which break them down into as many isolated parts as possible is needed. Furthermore, they reject the view that the parts are determined by the whole. They stress that there are phases in the development of any society when parts develop, not only in independence from the trends of the whole, but even in rebellion against them.[23]

There is no doubt that this fact is very important. It should not make us overlook, however, that the relationship between the whole and its parts is quite complicated and that even the forces which revolt against the whole are frequently still shaped and dominated by it.[24] This, in our opinion, is the reason why the movements we have described which aim at overcoming human estrangement do not fulfill their promise. They fail because they focus on isolated aspects of alienation and do not see them as interrelated parts of a trend that dominates contemporary society.

We respect the genuine concern which inspires the

search for remedies for special aspects of the problem of alienation, the attempts to initiate a religious renaissance, to reorient philosophic thought, to improve educational methods, and to stimulate stronger participation in the social and political challenges of our communities. But we cannot ignore the fact, which we have encountered again and again in our description of these attempts, that they leave the basis of human estrangement in society untouched. Preoccupied with overcoming some particular aspect of alienation, they have fallen prey to the very forces which they set forth to conquer.

As much as social scientists are opposed to the concept of "the whole of society," there is a growing realization among them that isolating abstractions which center around the economic man, the political man, the religious man, and so forth, are basically futile. Robert S. Lynd's important book, *Knowledge for What?* is an expression of the increasing dissatisfaction with a procedure which dismembers man's existence and activity into a number of seemingly separate realms. There is now more recognition of the fact that the understanding of man requires visualizing him as a whole, that social problems must be seen not as "jumbled details" but as "interacting parts in a single whole." In the field of criminology, for instance, various recent books have shown the inadequacy of attempts to trace crime to specific pathologies—personal or social—instead of tracing it to the foundation of society.[25] The problem of alienation too, we believe, can be adequately grasped only when it is understood as a part of the social situation as a whole.

To achieve an integrated view of social problems is no

easy task. So far the majority of social scientists have done little more than pay lip-service to it. They are not yet ready to give up the piecemeal approach which aims at isolating the economic, political, religious, sexual factors, and so on, at breaking down the social phenomenon under study into a large number of subdivisions—a procedure which, in Marx's words, shows how hard it is for scientists to transcend the patterns of alienated thinking. It would be wrong, however, to put the blame on the individual scholars, who are, as Lynd points out, "deeply committed, by training and by the need for security and advancement, to the official concepts, problems, and theoretical structure of [their] science."[26]

This piecemeal approach involves in practice avoiding problems of widespread change. Social scientists, as Lynd points out, "while subjecting themselves to the strain and risk of novelty in a given direction, . . . tend to hold everything else as fixed as possible."[27] This reluctance to accept change is not confined to those who work in the seclusion of their studies and are concerned with finding reliable and refined research methods. It is based on fears which have a grip on all of us, and which often prevent us from visualizing the direction in which our society is moving. This might be the reason why most social scientists, and many laymen, have been barred so far from an open-minded examination and thus from a genuine critique of Marx's and Tönnies' views on alienation. They sense that a thesis which describes contemporary man's alienation as growing out of the basic structure and direction of modern society invites a disturbing conclusion. There is no short-cut in our struggle against the forces of alienation. If we really want to triumph over them, we must accept the challenge to strive for a new foundation of society, for the development of economic and social institutions which will no longer be dominated by the commodity structure. Whether we believe with Marx that the achievement of this objective will require nationalization of the means of production, or whether we visualize with Tönnies the growth of cooperative enterprises (like those in the Scandinavian countries and Israel) as the foundation of a new society, in either case the change will have to go to the very roots of our social system.[28]

To emphasize the need for such a transformation does not mean to nourish the naive hope that it will automatically and forever do away with all the forces of alienation. Marx, it is true, rejected the attempt "to overcome alienation within the framework of alienation," to conquer alienation within a society geared to commodity relations. In a similar way Tönnies considered it impossible to revive *Gemeinschaft* within a society shaped by forces of *Gesellschaft*. But to derive from these negative statements the thesis that alienation will *necessarily* disappear after the structure of society has been changed, is to formulate a *non sequitur*. Marx and Tönnies, as we have seen, were certainly far from drawing such a conclusion. The socio-economic institutions which they envisaged as the foundation of the society of the future were for them nothing but a *condition* for the checkmating of tendencies toward alienation, a foothold from which the struggle could be waged.[29]

The recent history of Hungary and other East European countries offers tragic examples to make us aware that a social order which is not any longer directed by the predominance of commodity production may well fall prey to the forces of alienation. But wrong as it would be to belittle or to ignore these grim experiences, it would be equally wrong to ignore the lesson of history that basic changes require more than a few decades before they can produce their positive effects. Centuries of trial and error followed the rise of the Christian world and its struggle against the pagan civilizations of ancient times. Long periods of suffering had to be endured before the forces attacking the feudal rule and the guild system of the Middle Ages could result in the achievements of a free market economy and a society based on the rights of the individual. Only fools will expect that the emergence of a social order which is not any longer based on the commodity structure can produce its contributions to the fight against man's alienation without subjecting him to long periods of agony and pain.

This statement seems to strengthen the position of those who counsel against the social transformation which has been discussed in these pages. Why should we accept, they will ask, all the anguish which accompanies a fundamental change of our social institutions, when even a social order which is not any longer based on commodity production does not offer any certainty, but merely a chance, for realizing man's dream of escaping from his state of estrangement? The appeal of this way of reasoning will be strong. Individuals, as well as societies, are haunted by deep fears when they face the need for basic change. Most of us prefer to cling to the old and known state of things. We would rather endure its familiar inadequacies than launch on an adventurous new start with promises which are uncertain and realizable only at exacting costs. The prevalence of this attitude is a fact which no measure of wishful thinking can dispute away. But to reckon with it does not mean to ignore the alternative which is shaping up for those who feel we must tackle the problem of alienation. Either we dare take the risk and strive for a new stage of human history in which man, though not overcoming all phases of alienation, will at least have a chance to struggle against the economic and social ones; or we shrink back from the dangers which a transformation of the social order might engender. If we choose the latter course we must resign ourselves to living in a world in which the tendencies which separate man from his fellow man, from the life that surrounds him, and even from himself, will continue unabated. Opposition to this estrangement will amount to nothing but an empty protest; and at best remedies will be found that do not come to grips with the forces of alienation, but merely heal some of the wounds which they inflict upon us.

NOTES

1. Simmel's importance for present day sociology has been described by Nicholas J. Spykman in *The Social Theory of Georg Simmel*. See also Rudolf Heberle's article "The Sociology of Georg Simmel: The Forms of Social Interaction." Simmel's influence is shown in Lewis Coser's recent book *The Functions of Social Conflict*. In past years the Free Press has published a large part of Simmel's sociological works in English translation. The titles are listed in the Bibliography following these notes.

2. Georg Simmel, *Die Religion,* esp. pp. 28-29.

3. *Kierkegaard's Concluding Unscientific Postscript,* pp. 281, 319, 177. Feuerbach, "Grundsätze der Philosophie der Zukunft," section 51. In selecting Kierkegaard's and Feuerbach's statements we have followed Paul Tillich's article "Existential Philosophy," to which we are indebted in many ways.

4. Ludwig Binswanger, *Ausgewählte Vorträge & Aufsätze,* p. 15.

5. Jean-Paul Sartre, *The Republic of Silence,* pp. 498-499.

6. José Ortega y Gasset, "History As A System," p. 213, also p. 216.

7. Jean-Paul Sartre, *L'Etre et le Néant,* pp. 515, 111.

8. Werner Brock's introduction to *Existence and Being* by Martin Heidegger, p. 56. This book gives the English translation of four essays by Heidegger.

9. The introduction to Simmel's book *Philosophische Kultur* offers an example of this attitude. Here Simmel states that man, in spite of all his efforts, has not yet found the answer to many questions which have troubled him for thousands of years. Simmel, however, urges us not to get discouraged and invites us to ponder the meaning of the following fable. On his deathbed a farmer tells his children that a treasure of great value lies buried in the fields belonging to the family. Upon their return from the father's grave the sons begin to plough the land. They dig in vain. The treasure remains undiscovered. Only the following year, when they realize that as a result of their arduous and seemingly futile efforts the soil has become enriched and yields a threefold harvest of fruit, do they understand what their father meant when he hinted at hidden wealth. According to Simmel the fable symbolizes the challenge to the human mind. We must go on groping for answers, even if the treasure can never be unearthed and even if there should not be any treasure. For only by ploughing the soil in which knowledge and wisdom can grow will the human mind fulfill itself and attain the enrichment it is destined to attain.

10. Martin Heidegger, *Ueber den Humanismus,* p. 27. Rainer Maria Rilke, "Herbsttag" (Autumn Day). We have followed but slightly modified C. F. MacIntyre's translation, p. 37.

11. From the poem "Die grosse Nacht." Our translation differs from that of Leishman, p. 109. Bollnow refers to this and other poems by Rilke in order to show the link

between this poet's work and some of the central ideas of existential philosophy. See his *Existenzphilosophie,* pp. 39-40.

12. *The Love Letters of Phyllis McGinley,* p. 37.

13. Kafka's letter, written December 16, 1911, is mentioned in Erich Heller's book *The Disinherited Mind,* p. 157.

14. Thomas Wolfe, "The Return of the Prodigal," p. 120.

15. Arthur Miller, *Death of a Salesman,* pp. 65, 56, 64, 135, 119-120.

Notes to Chapter Two

1. Romano Guardini, *Die Macht,* p. 10.

2. This development is one of the main themes of Carl L. Becker's book *The Heavenly City of the Eighteenth-Century Philosophers,* especially the chapters "Climates of Opinion" and "The Laws of Nature and of Nature's God." See also Alfred Meusel, *Untersuchungen über das Erkenntnisobjekt bei Marx,* pp. 95-96.

3. Gottfried Traub, *Ethik und Kapitalismus,* pp. 91, 75, 92, 90. For a discussion of Traub's ideas and of the changing attitudes toward technology see Hans Freyer, *Die Bewertung der Wirtschaft im philosophischen Denken des 19. Jahrhunderts,* esp. Chapter IX.

4. E. J. Hobsbawm in his article "The Machine Breakers" examines the scope and the impact of these riots. See also F. O. Darvall, *Popular Disturbances and Public Order in Regency England.* Among earlier works dealing with these events we mention: G. von Schulze-

Gaevernitz, *Social Peace. A Study of the Trade Union Movement in England,* Chapter V, "Class Warfare"; Werner Sombart, *Socialism and the Social Movement,* Part II, Chapter I, "The Early History of the Social Movement"; Sidney and Beatrice Webb, *Industrial Democracy,* Chapter VIII, "New Processes and Machinery." Still valuable as an interpretation of the economic and social character of the period is Arnold Toynbee's *Lectures on the Industrial Revolution in England,* particularly Chapter VIII, "The Chief Features of the Revolution," and Chapter IX, "The Growth of Pauperism," and the address of 1881, "Industry and Democracy," included in the second part of the book. This speech has been omitted in the paperback edition by the Beacon Press 1956. Important material about the conditions during the industrial revolution can also be found in E. J. Hobsbawm's article "The British Standard of Living 1790-1850," and in Maurice Dobb's book *Studies in the Development of Capitalism,* Chapter VII, "The Industrial Revolution and the Nineteenth Century."

5. See Marx, *Capital* (Moore/Aveling translation), Vol. I, Ch. XV, Section 5, "The Strife Between Workman and Machinery," pp. 467-468. Veblen and other writers have shown that even in our present economy the application of new technological devices occasionally encounters a certain resistance on the part of some groups who believe that the use of newly developed production methods are conflicting with their vested interests. See Thorstein Veblen *The Vested Interests and the State of the Industrial Arts,* especially Chapter V, "The Vested Interests," pp. 93-94; *The Instinct of Workmanship and the State of Industrial Arts,* especially Ch. VII, "The Machine Industry," pp. 344 ff; *The Engineers and the Price System,* particularly the first three chapters, "On

the Nature and Uses of Sabotage," "The Industrial System and the Captains of Industry," and "The Captains of Finance and the Engineers." See also the study *Technological Trends and National Policy* issued by the National Resources Committee, Part I, Section IV, pp. 39-66, "Resistances to the Adoption of Technological Innovations."

6. The first of these titles is listed in the Bibliography under Rencontres Internationales de Genève 1947; the second under Georges Gurvitch (editor); the third under Romano Guardini.

7. Max Weber spoke of this loss, of "the elimination of magic from the world," as a process occurring throughout history and particularly in the modern world. See Max Weber, *The Protestant Ethic and the Spirit of Capitalism,* p. 221, note 19. This aspect of technological development has been analyzed by Herbert Marcuse in his masterly article "Some Social Implications of Modern Technology." See especially pp. 420-421. Our description owes much to Marcuse's paper.

8. Romano Guardini, *Die Macht,* p. 55.

Notes to Chapter Three

1. *The World of Yesterday,* Ch. XVI, "The Agony of Peace," pp. 412, 411.

2. Samuel A. Stouffer, *Communism, Conformity, and Civil Liberties. A Cross-Section of the Nation Speaks its Mind.* See Chapter III, "Is There a National Anxiety Neurosis?", p. 59. *Look Magazine,* which brought out part of the book before its publication, called the project "one of the most searching public opinion

surveys ever conducted in the United States." See *Look Magazine*, March 22, 1955, pp. 25 ff.

3. *From Max Weber: Essays in Sociology*, Ch. IV, "Politics as a Vocation," especially pp. 125-126.

4. Georg W. F. Hegel, *The Philosophy of History*, p. 31.

5. *New York Times*, March 11, 1955.

6. *New York Herald Tribune*, August 22, 1954.

7. For an excellent description of the role which this assumption and its underlying "ameliorative" attitude play in the social sciences and especially in much of present-day research work on economic problems see Robert S. Lynd, *Knowledge For What?*, Chapter IV, "The Social Sciences As Tools," especially pp. 119, 144 ff.

8. Malcolm Cowley, *The Literary Situation*, p. 83.

9. Stouffer, *Communism, Conformity, and Civil Liberties*, pp. 59-60, 73. The movement from the public to the private is not confined to the United States. Helmut Schelsky, a West German sociologist, describes it as basic to the outlook of German youth, whom he portrays as answering the call to participate in public organizations, or even in youth groups, with the indifferent reply "ohne uns" (without us). To characterize this attitude he creates a bold new term "privatistisch." See his comprehensive and much discussed book *Die Skeptische Generation. Eine Soziologie der deutschen Jugend*, espec. pp. 91 ff.

10. *The New York Times Magazine*, August 9, 1953.

Notes to Chapter Four

1. Among recent papers which express skepticism toward a quantifying approach we mention the following: François Bourricaud, "Sur la Prédominance de l'Analyse Microscopique dans la Sociologie Américaine Contemporaine"; S. M. Lipset and R. Bendix, "Social Status and Social Structure: A Reexamination of Data and Interpretations"; Bernard Rosenberg and Norman D. Humphrey, "The Secondary Nature of the Primary Group." For the view which accepts in principle the quantifying approach but recognizes the need for self-criticism, see Samuel A. Stouffer's presidential address "Measurement in Sociology" at the 1953 meeting of the American Sociological Society.

2. We refer the reader especially to the following books and papers: Christopher Dawson, "Sociology as a Science"; Robert S. Lynd, *Knowledge For What? The Place of Social Science in American Culture;* Jules Monnerot, *Les Faits Sociaux Ne Sont Pas des Choses;* Thomas Humphrey Marshall, *Sociology at the Crossroads;* Behice Boran, "Sociology in Retrospect"; Robert Redfield, "The Art of Social Science"; Edward Shils, *The Present State of American Sociology;* Reinhard Bendix, *Social Science and the Distrust of Reason;* Herbert Blumer, "What is Wrong with Social Theory?"; Howard Becker, "Vitalizing Sociological Theory"; Florian Znaniecki, "Basic Problems of Contemporary Sociology."

3. Florian Znaniecki, "Basic Problems of Contemporary Sociology," p. 520. Dissatisfaction with the situation described by Znaniecki has stimulated some recent efforts to integrate structural and functional analysis

of social phenomena. The most significant of these attempts is to be found in the work undertaken by Talcott Parsons and his school. See especially Talcott Parsons & Edward A. Shils, *Toward a General Theory of Action;* Parsons, *The Social System;* Parsons, *Essays in Sociological Theory;* M. J. Levy, Jr., *The Structure of Society.* Whether Parsons' and his followers' approach to the problem can be considered satisfactory is still a controversial question. The claims of this school have recently been challenged by a number of American and European sociologists, among whom we mention the following: Barrington Moore, Jr., "The New Scholasticism and the Study of Politics," esp. pp. 100 ff; Barrington Moore, Jr., "Strategy in Social Science, esp. pp. 125 ff.; G. E. Swanson, "The Approach to a General Theory of Action by Parsons & Shils"; Alain Touraine, "Review of Parsons & Shils"; Wayne Hield, "The Study of Change in Social Science"; David Lockwood, "Some Remarks on 'The Social System' "; Ralf Dahrendorf, "Out of Utopia: Toward a Reorientation of Sociological Analysis." Bernard Barber gives a critical appraisal of some objections to Parsons' concepts in his article "Structural-Functional Analysis."

Another attempt to develop a theory on the relationship between the structure and function of society has been presented by Joyce O. Hertzler in his book *Society in Action. A Study of Basic Social Processes.* This work has been paid considerably less attention in recent sociological literature than the contributions of Parsons and his followers.

4. The inability of leading scholars to visualize contemporary society as a whole in the perspective of change has been described by Paul M. Sweezy in his article "Toynbee's Universal History."

5. Tönnies presented a draft of his book in 1881 when he was appointed to the Department of Philosophy at the University of Kiel. After its publication, in 1887, among the few who expressed their appreciation of it were the philosophers Harald Höffding, Paul Barth, and Friedrich Paulsen, and the economists Adolph Wagner and Gustav Schmoller. One of the first American reviews appeared in 1897, in the second volume of the *American Journal of Sociology*. The author, Dr. O. Thon, turned against the mood of despair which he believed he discerned in Tönnies' concepts but recognized that the book "must be reckoned among the most profound and suggestive of all times."

An English translation appeared in 1941 under the title *Fundamental Concepts of Sociology (Gemeinschaft und Gesellschaft)* translated and supplemented by Charles P. Loomis (quoted hereafter as *Fundamental Concepts*). Another edition was published in 1957. Loomis' valuable introduction gives a description of Tönnies' personality and work. This introduction has been amplified in the edition of 1957. It includes a section by John C. McKinney, in collaboration with Loomis, which relates *Gemeinschaft und Gesellschaft* to typologies developed by authors like Durkheim, Cooley, Redfield, Becker, Sorokin, Weber, and Parsons. It also describes an attempt to apply Tönnies' categories and classifications, in a modified way, to the study of rural communities in Costa Rica.

6. Tönnies, *Fundamental Concepts,* p. 74 (1957 ed., p. 65).

7. Tönnies, *Fundamental Concepts,* pp. 74, 88 (1957 ed., pp. 65, 77).

8. See Morris Janowitz, *The Community Press in an Urban Setting,* esp. p. 17; Daniel Bell, "The Theory

of Mass Society. A Critique"; Edward A. Shils, "Daydreams and Nightmares: Reflections on the Criticism of Mass Culture," esp. p. 599; Edward A. Shils, "Primordial, Personal, Sacred and Civil Ties. Some Particular Observations on the Relationship of Sociological Research and Theory," esp. pp. 131-133. Bell states: "There are in the United States today at least 200,000 voluntary organizations, associations, clubs, societies, lodges, and fraternities with an aggregate (but obviously overlapping) membership of close to eighty million men and women." (p. 80). However the widely held notion that Americans are a nation of joiners is, according to recent studies, a generalization that does not bear close scrutiny. See, for example, Charles R. Wright and Herbert H. Hyman "Voluntary Association Memberships of American Adults: Evidence from National Sample Surveys."

9. Tönnies, *Fundamental Concepts,* p. 15, note 1 (1957 ed., p. 284, note 1); p. 119 (1957 ed., p. 103).

10. J. A. Hobson, *Work and Wealth,* pp. 25-26.

11. Tönnies, *Fundamental Concepts,* p. 186, (1957 ed., p. 162).

12. Tönnies, *Thomas Hobbes. Leben und Lehre,* p. 265.

13. David Riesman, *The Lonely Crowd,* p. 14.

14. Harald Höffding, *Mindre Arbejder,* pp. 142-157, esp. p. 144.

15. Georg Lukács, *Die Zerstörung der Vernunft,* p. 468; Georg Lukács, "Die Deutsche Soziologie vor dem ersten Weltkrieg," p. 480.

16. Tönnies, *Fundamental Concepts,* pp. 194-195, note 1. (1957 ed., pp. 169-170, note 1). We have slightly changed Loomis' translation.

17. Tönnies, "Zur Einleitung in die Soziologie," pp. 65-74, especially p. 71. In a footnote to the statement quoted in the text Tönnies remarks that he is proud to have referred to the importance of Marxian concepts when he wrote *Gemeinschaft und Gesellschaft,* "since in 1887 it was still unheard of to recognize or to actually make special mention of the significance of Marx for sociological theory."

18. See the preface to the first edition of *Gemeinschaft und Gesellschaft,* reprinted in *Soziologische Studien und Kritiken,* Erste Sammlung, p. 43.

19. Tönnies, *Marx. Leben und Lehre,* pp. x, 145.

20. Tönnies, *Einführung in die Soziologie,* pp. 269-283, esp. pp. 270-271; Marx: *A Contribution to the Critique of Political Economy,* p. 11. See also Rudolf Heberle, "The Sociological System of Ferdinand Tönnies," pp. 227-248, esp. p. 241. Heberle emphasizes that for Tönnies "the economic interpretation of history was a useful device of analysis but not the last word in wisdom." See further Albert Salomon: "In Memoriam Ferdinand Tönnies (1855-1936)". After having described the affinity between Marx's and Tönnies' concepts, Salomon adds: "This agreement with the fundamental ideas of Marx, does not, however, make Tönnies a Marxist." (p. 355).

21. Tönnies, "Sozialreform ehedem und heute," pp. 664-665. Also his Autobiographical Sketch, esp. p. 231, and his Preface to the Third Edition of *Gemeinschaft und Gesellschaft,* in his *Soziologische Studien und Kritiken,* Erste Sammlung, pp. 63-64.

22. Tönnies, *Das Eigentum,* p. 12. Tönnies wrote this study against the background of the plebiscite held in Germany during the Weimar Republic to decide the question of the expropriation of the German princes, dethroned in November 1918. Tönnies expressed his views on the historical and social basis of private property in many of his writings. See for example, *Einführung in die Soziologie,* pp. 156-165; and "Entwicklung der Soziologie in Deutschland im 19. Jahrhundert," esp. pp. 95 ff.

23. The *Economic-Philosophical Manuscripts* of 1844 were first published in 1932 in the Marx-Engels *Gesamtausgabe;* and in the same year in a collection of Marx's and Engels' early writings on historical materialism compiled by S. Landshut and J. P. Mayer. In 1950 a further edition of the Manuscripts appeared under the title *Nationalökonomie und Philosophie* with an introductory essay by Erich Thier. Until recently only parts of the *Economic-Philosophical Manuscripts* were translated into English. See the mimeographed pamphlet *Selected essays from the Oekonomisch-Philosophische Manuskripte* translated by Ria Stone, New York, 1947. See also *Karl Marx. Selected Writings in Sociology and Social Philosophy* edited by T. B. Bottomore and Maximilien Rubel, especially Part III, Section 4 and Part V.

The *Oekonomische Studien* of 1844 and 1845 were first published in 1932 in the Marx-Engels *Gesamtausgabe.* They consist mainly of annotated excerpts from a large number of writings by British, French and German economists and have not yet been translated.

24. Marx, *Oekonomische Studien,* pp. 536, 544; Marx, "Zur Judenfrage," p. 584 (Landshut, p. 182, Stenning's translation, p. 56).

25. Marx, "Zur Judenfrage," pp. 584-586, 594 (Stenning's translation, pp. 57-59, 74). See also Marx, "Kritik des Hegelschen Staatsrechts," pp. 436, 497; Marx, *The Poverty of Philosophy*, p. 84; Marx to Ruge May 1843, p. 561. Marx's use of the terms *Gemeinschaft* and *Gesellschaft* in his letter to Ruge anticipates the distinction later made by Tönnies.

26. F. H. Heinemann, *Existentialism and the Modern Predicament*, p. 12. In his recent article "Alienation and Community" Charles Taylor has shown the central importance of the concept of alienation in Marx's work and the failure of many of his followers to recognize the significance of this idea. Many of Taylor's points are corroborated and illustrated in Stuart Hall's essay "A Sense of Classlessness". We want to refer the reader to these valuable contributions, which appeared after the completion of our manuscript.

27. Marx, *Oekonomisch-Philosophische Manuskripte*, pp. 156, 165; Kierkegaard, *Concluding Unscientific Postscript*, pp. 278-279.

28. Marx, *Oekonomisch-Philosophische Manuskripte*, p. 141; Marx, *Oekonomische Studien*, p. 536. In the following pages we discuss only one cardinal aspect of Marx's theory of alienation—the impact of commodity structure. However he traced alienation also to the division of labor and to the power of the state, two forces in society which he saw as closely related to commodity production, especially in the modern world. See the comprehensive summary of Marx's concept of alienation which Stanley W. Moore gives in his book *The Critique of Capitalist Democracy*, esp. pp. 124 ff.

29. Marx, *Capital*, Vol. 1, p. 44. On the role of commodities see also Marx, *Theories of Surplus Value* p. 170.

John R. Commons, the American scholar whose work contributed so much to the understanding of the economic and social significance of legal institutions, has stated: ". . . the transition in the meaning of property from the use-value to the exchange-value of things, and therefore from the producing power that increases use-values to the bargaining power that increases exchange-values, is more than a transition—it is a reversal." *Legal Foundations of Capitalism,* p. 21.

30. See Marx, *Capital,* Vol. 1, p. 100; Marx, *A Contribution To The Critique Of Political Economy,* p. 53. Compare the remark of Commons: "The reversal [of use value and exchange value] was not at first important when business was small and weak—it becomes important when Capitalism rules the world." *Legal Foundations of Capitalism,* p. 21.

A psychologist as critical of Marx as Erich Fromm has recognized the great impact of the commodity on the emotional structures of modern man. See the section "The Marketing Orientation" in his book *Man For Himself. An Inquiry Into The Psychology of Ethics,* pp. 67 ff. Fromm states correctly that "the marketing orientation developed as a dominant one only in the modern era." In emphasizing this fact he refers to Karl Polanyi, who has described the difference between the modern market economy an¹ the individual acts of barter which "are common in almost all types of primitive society, but . . . are considered as incidental since they do not provide for the necessaries of life." See Karl Polanyi, *The Great Transformation,* p. 61. For Fromm's criticism of Marx's theories see his book *The Sane Society,* pp. 253-269.

31. Marx, *Oekonomisch-Philosophische Manuskripte,* pp. 118, 120; Marx, *Oekonomische Studien,* p. 545.

32. Marx and Engels, *The Communist Manifesto,* Section I; Marx, *Oekonomische Studien,* p. 545.

33. Marx, *Oekonomisch-Philosophische Manuskripte,* p. 128.

34. Marx, *Oekonomisch-Philosophische Manuskripte,* pp. 127-128.

35. Marx, *Capital,* Vol. 1 (Moore/Aveling translation), p. 195; Marx, *Oekonomisch-Philosophische Manuskripte,* p. 63. See also Marx, *The Poverty of Philosophy,* p. 47, where Marx points out that the only thing considered in the capitalist work process is time, that is, the number of hours for which the laborer has to be paid. "Time is everything, man is nothing; he is at the most, time's carcase."

36. Marx, *Capital,* Vol. 1 (Eden and Cedar Paul translation), p. 381. We have quoted from this edition of *Capital* since the translation by Moore and Aveling (p. 396) does not seem fully satisfactory.

37. Marx, *Capital,* Vol. 1 (Moore/Aveling translation), pp. 461-462, 389.

38. Marx, *Oekonomisch-Philosophische Manuskripte,* p. 88 (Stone translation, p. 12).

39. Marx, *Oekonomisch-Philosophische Manuskripte,* pp. 85-86 (Stone translation, pp. 10-11).

40. Marx, *Oekonomisch-Philosophische Manuskripte,* pp. 83-84, 88 (Stone translation, pp. 9, 12).

41. Marx, *Oekonomisch-Philosophische Manuskripte,* p. 97.

42. The text of the Clayton Act can be found in *Documents of American History,* edited by Henry Steele Commager, Vol. II. The text of the Treaty of Versailles can be found in *Supplement to the American Journal of International Law,* Vol. 13, Number 3, July 1919: Official Documents, p. 375.

43. Emil Lederer and Jakob Marschak, "Die Klassen auf dem Arbeitsmarkt und ihre Organisationen," esp. p. 112; W. V. Owen, *Labor Problems,* p. 31.

The protest against this attitude toward labor was one of the central themes of the social gospel movement. In an address given in 1886 The Rt. Rev. Henry C. Potter turned against "the fallacy which may be true enough in the domain of political economy, but is essentially false in the domain of religion, *that labor and the laborer are alike a commodity,* to be bought and sold, employed or dismissed, paid or underpaid as the market shall decree." *Christian Thought,* Fourth Series, edited by Charles T. Deems, pp. 289 ff. For further sources concerning this aspect of the social gospel see Sidney Fine, *Laissez Faire and the General Welfare-State. A Study of Conflict in American Thought 1865-1901,* Chapter VI. esp. p. 175; Charles Howard Hopkins, *The Rise of the Social Gospel in American Protestantism 1865-1915,* esp. Chapter V.

44. Marx and Engels, *Die Heilige Familie,* p. 206. See also the editor's note to Marx and Engels, *The German Ideology,* edited by R. Pascal, pp. 202-203.

45. Marx, "Debatten über Pressfreiheit," pp. 222-223. Mannheim's trust in the role of the intellectuals is shared by many, including some of his opponents. Charles Frankel, whose book *The Case For Modern Man* is highly critical of Mannheim, states that "the only effective world community that now exists is the community

of science." (p. 143). These words seem less to describe actual conditions than to formulate a desirable objective. We still live in a world where cleavages between those committed to the pursuit of truth are deep. Scholars seldom rise above the conflicts between nations and classes. They are often embroiled in clashes between differing schools of thought. Communication between them is hampered by arbitrarily constructed terminologies intelligible only to the initiated. To achieve the community of which Frankel speaks intellectuals would have to attain a degree of outer and inner freedom still sorely lacking.

46. *Saturday Review,* July 28, 1956. An illustration of the shock method is Mary McCarthy's story "Dottie Makes An Honest Woman of Herself." "Get yourself a pessary . . ." are the words with which the story opens; the young man who gives this advice to his new girl friend adds by way of explanation: "A female contraceptive, a plug, . . ." *Partisan Review,* often considered representative of the intellectual climate of the American writer, a few months later published Leslie A. Fiedler's "Pull Down Vanity," a story which outdoes Miss McCarthy in the use of shocks.

47. This example is given by Georg Lukács in his book *Karl Marx und Friedrich Engels als Literaturhistoriker,* pp. 210-211. For an English translation of Schnitzler's play see Bibliography.

48. Romano Guardini, *Die Macht,* pp. 117-118.

49. William Faulkner, "On Privacy; The American Dream: What Happened To It?", pp. 35-37.

50. Arthur Twining Hadley, *Economic Problems of Democracy,* pp. 143-144.

Notes to Chapter Five

1. Romano Guardini, *Die Macht*, p. 55. See above Chapter II, "Technology and Alienation," p. 42.

2. Gunther Anders, "The World as Phantom and as Matrix," pp. 19, 22.

3. *Ibid*, p. 20.

4. Quoted from the *New York Times*, September 7, 1956.

5. Elizabeth Ellis Hoyt, *Consumption in our Society*, pp. 301-302.

6. Paul Tillich, *Biblical Religion and the Search for Ultimate Reality*, p. 55. Miguel de Unamuno's book *Del Sentimiento Trágico de la Vida* (1912) did not find a widely spread response in the first decades after its publication, but it now exercises a strong influence in many parts of the world.

7. Paul Tillich, *Der Mensch im Christentum und im Marxismus*, pp. 13-14.

8. Ernst Troeltsch, *Augustin, die christliche Antike und das Mittelalter*, esp. pp. 1-7, 157-173.

9. See Maurice Dobb, *Studies in the Development of Capitalism*, Chapter III, esp. pp. 116-117.

10. Marc Bloch, *La Société Féodale. La Formation des Liens de Dépendance*, pp. 402-405; George C. Homans, *English Villagers of the Thirteenth Century*, esp. pp. 268-269, 346-349. Also Karl Marx, *Capital* Vol. III, Ch. XLVII, Section II, "Labor Rent," esp. p. 918; Maurice Dobb, *Studies in the Development of Capitalism*, p. 36;

P. Boissonnade, *Life and Work in Medieval Europe (Fifth to Fifteenth Centuries)*, pp. 117-332.

Bloch's description should not be understood as an attempt to idealize the age of feudalism. He is well aware of the fact that "the feudal regime never ceased to contain a great number of constraints, violences and abuses." See his article "European Feudalism," esp. p. 204. Readers who consider Bloch's position inconsistent should bear in mind the complexity of the feudal system, which included a great number of variations and disparities. There were, for example, important distinctions between the serfs. Boissonnade has stated: "There were . . . degrees of serfdom and a whole hierarchy of serfs." (*op. cit.* p. 137.) The conditions of the villeins, who enjoyed more personal and economic liberties, contrasted markedly with those of the rest of the serfs. (*ibid.* pp. 132 ff.) Moreover there were local differences, often so deep that a recent author has stated: "No picture of the manorial system can be strictly accurate, because conditions varied so much in different places." (Leo Huberman, *Man's Worldly Goods. The Story of the Wealth of Nations*, p. 8.) Finally we must keep in mind the dissimilarities between the various historical stages of feudalism. A detailed description of them can be found in Dobb, *op. cit.* pp. 37 ff.

11. This point has been made forcefully by Herbert Marcuse, who has argued that the present must be "measured not in terms of past stages, but in terms of its own possibilities." See his book *Eros and Civilization. A Philosophical Inquiry into Freud*, pp. 101-102. See also his lecture "Die Idee des Fortschritts im Lichte der Psychoanalyse," esp. p. 439. The importance of Marcuse's argument has been stressed by Barrington Moore, Jr. in his essay "Totalitarian Elements in Pre-Industrial Societies," esp. p. 32.

12. Marx, *Oekonomisch-Philosophische Manuskripte,* p. 126. We have used the translation in *Karl Marx, Selected Writings in Sociology and Social Philosophy,* edited by T. B. Bottomore and Maximilien Rubel. Marx, *Capital,* Vol. III. pp. 954-955. Italics have been added; minor changes in the translation have been made.

13. Tönnies, *Einführung in die Soziologie,* p. 239.

14. Stanley Rowland, Jr., "Suburbia Buys Religion," p. 79. Concern about this development has been expressed in many theological writings. See Will Herberg, *Protestant-Catholic-Jew. An Essay in American Religious Sociology,* esp. Chapter V. See also Nathan Glazer's discussion of this book in the *New Republic,* November 14, 1955.

15. See Martin Heidegger's lecture "Wozu Dichter?" esp. p. 271; Martin Heidegger "Was ist Metaphysik?", pp. 44-45 (English translation, pp. 388-389).

16. These figures are taken from an editorial entitled "Is Your Child Surplus?" in the *New York Times,* February 26, 1957. The statistics presented by the U. S. Office of Education have been questioned by the education department of the United States Chamber of Commerce. See the *New York Times,* March 2, 1957.

17. Quoted from the *Boston Daily Globe,* June 17, 1955. Italics in original.

18. Arnold A. Rogow, "The Educational Malaise," p. 71.

19. The expectation attached to these appointments is indicated by an editorial in the *New York Times* after Dr. Robert Francis Goheen had been made president of

Princeton University: "The selection of Dr. Goheen was significant, quite apart from his personal qualifications, in that the board of trustees deliberately chose a humanist to lead the university in this age of specialization and of the machine." (December 14, 1956.) We can assume that the trustees of Harvard University were guided by similar motives when, upon the resignation of James B. Conant, a scientist, they selected Nathan D. Pusey, a student of classical languages, as president.

20. James Bryce, *The American Commonwealth*, Vol. II., p. 491; Vol. I, p. 343.

21. "Decay at the city's core has laid the foundation of new decay on the city's periphery." This statement was made by H. Warren Dunham in "The City: A Problem in Equilibrium and Control," p. 162. Among the many valuable contributions in the same collection in which this lecture is published we mention "Political Apathy —Functions of Urban Transition," by Joseph D. Lohman. The failure to decentralize is more surprising for Bryce's present-day followers than it would have been for the British scholar himself. In spite of his praise of self-governing administrative units, Bryce had no illusions about the relative strength of "centripetal" and " centrifugal" forces in government. He stated realistically that in the modern world "the more normal tendency to aggregation and centralization prevails." *The American Commonwealth*, Vol. II, pp. 709-710.

22. William H. Whyte Jr., *The Organization Man*, p. 287. See also A. C. Spectorsky, *The Exurbanites*; John Keats, *The Crack in the Picture Window;* The Editors of Fortune, *The Exploding Metropolis.*

23. See S. F. Nadel, *The Theory of Social Structure*, p. 3.

24. This view was often expressed by Wilhelm Dilthey. Especially in his studies on the concept of historical eras and epochs he stressed the idea that each force which sets itself in opposition to the prevailing trends of an age remains bound by the age. Wilhelm Dilthey, "Der Aufbau der geschichtlichen Welt in den Geisteswissenschaften," p. 178.

25. Robert S. Lynd, *Knowledge for What?*, p. 50. In the field of criminology we refer particularly to the classic study *White Collar Crime* by the late Edwin H. Sutherland. See esp. Chapters I and XV.

26. Karl Marx, *Oekonomisch-Philosophische Manuskripte*, p. 132. Robert S. Lynd, *Knowledge for What?*, pp. 17-18.

27. *Ibid.*

28. How difficult it is for most of us to accept this fact and to draw the necessary conclusions from it is illustrated by the work of Erich Fromm. What made *Man For Himself* so important was the understanding of the relationship between market economy and alienation. This insight, however, seems to have influenced very little the proposals which his later book *The Sane Society* presents for overcoming alienation. His suggestions center around the hope to revive the spirit of "humanistic communitarianism." He proposes measures to counteract the trend toward centralization in industry, to provide the worker with a higher degree of technological and economic knowledge, to establish discussion groups of management, workers, and consumers in order to secure "co-management and workers' participation," and so on. Fromm seems to have sensed the inadequacy of these approaches to the problem of alienation. It is noteworthy that though a determined

critic of Marxian socialism, he is compelled to add (though cautiously) some hints of the need for institutional changes, including "a certain degree of direct state intervention and socialization." (pp. 331, 333).

Herbert Marcuse has attacked the theoretical position which led Fromm to his revision of Freudian concepts. He describes it as thinking which directs "criticism against surface phenomena, while accepting the basic premises of the criticized society." See his "Critique of Neo-Freudian Revisionism," the epilogue to his *Eros and Civilization,* esp. p. 261. See also the continuation of this discussion in Fromm's article "The Human Implications of Instinctivistic 'Radicalism'," Marcuse's "A Reply to Erich Fromm," and finally Fromm's "A Counter Rebuttal." The present controversy between two schools of Freudian thought does not concern us here; yet we want to express our agreement with Marcuse's recognition of the difficult plight of individuals who strive for the productive realization of the personality, who try to take seriously the values stressed by Fromm such as responsibility, respect for one's fellow man, productive love and happiness, and who want to "remain sane and full of 'well being' in a society . . . . dominated by the commodity relations of the 'market.' " *Eros and Civilization,* pp. 258-259.

29. See Marx and Engels, *Die Heilige Familie,* p. 213. In this work Marx and Engels urge us to do away with alienation, not just in theoretical discussions, but also by changing actual conditions, so that not only in the realm of pure thought but also in his real existence man may become human. (pp. 223-224.)

Bibliography

IF WE LISTED all the literature which indirectly or explicitly explores the many facets of alienation, our bibliography would be excessively long. Therefore we note primarily the books and articles to which the text and footnotes refer. Only a few other writings, marked by asterisks, have been added. A number of them present interpretations of alienation which differ from ours. Others, like those of Georg Lukács, Herbert Marcuse, Karl Löwith, and Robert Heiss, have been included because they have contributed much to the position from which this essay has been written. Some philosophical and religious contributions have been mentioned, because they show that even the thinking of non-Marxists has been stirred by Marx's description of the alienation of modern man.

* ACTON, H. B.	*The Illusion of the Epoch: Marxism-Leninism as a Philosophical Creed.* London, Cohen & West Ltd., 1955.
* ADAMS, H. P.	*Karl Marx in his Earlier Writings.* London, George Allen & Unwin Ltd., 1940.
ANDERS, GUNTHER	"The World as Phantom and as Matrix," *Dissent* (Winter 1956).
* ARENDT, HANNAH	*The Human Condition.* Chicago, Chicago University Press, 1958.
* BAERWALD, FRIEDRICH	"A Sociological View of Depersonalization," *Thought,* Fordham University Quarterly, Vol. XXXI, No. 120 (Spring 1956).
BARBER, BERNARD	"Structural-Functional Analysis," *American Sociological Review* (April 1956).

BARRETT, GEORGE — "Portrait of the Korean Veteran," *The New York Times Magazine*, August 9, 1953.

* BARTH, HANS — *Wahrheit und Ideologie*. Zürich, Manesse Verlag, Conzett & Huber, 1945.

BECKER, CARL L. — *The Heavenly City of the Eighteenth-Century Philosophers*. New Haven, Yale University Press, Eighth Printing, 1951.

BECKER, HOWARD — "Vitalizing Sociological Theory," *American Sociological Review*, Vol. XIX (August 1954).

BELL, DANIEL — "The Theory of Mass Society: A Critique," *Commentary* (July 1956).

BENDIX, REINHARD — *Social Science and the Distrust of Reason*. University of California Publications in Sociology and Social Institutions, Vol. I, No. 1. Berkeley, University of California Press, 1951.

————————AND
LIPSET, S. M. — See LIPSET, S. M.

BINSWANGER, LUDWIG — *Ausgewählte Vorträge & Aufsätze*. Bern, Francke, 1947.

BLOCH, MARC — "European Feudalism," *Encyclopedia of the Social Sciences*, Vol. VI.

———————— — *La Société Féodale: La Formation des Liens de Dépendence*. Paris, Editions Albin Michel, 1949.

BLUMER, HERBERT — "What is Wrong with Social Theory?," *American Sociological Review*, Vol. XIX (February 1954).

BOISSONNADE, P. — *Life and Work in Medieval Europe (Fifth to Fifteenth Centuries)*. New York, Alfred A. Knopf, 1927.

BOLLNOW, OTTO FRIEDRICH — *Existenzphilosophie*. Stuttgart, W. Kohlhammer Verlag, 3rd Edition, 1949.

BORAN, BEHICE "Sociology in Retrospect," *The American Journal of Sociology,* Vol. LII, No. 4 (January 1947).

BOURRICAUD, FRANÇOIS "Sur la Prédominance de l'Analyse Microscopique dans la Sociologie Américaine Contemporaine," *Cahiers Internationaux de Sociologie,* Vol. XIII Cahier Double. Septième Année. 1952.

* BRAYBROOKE, DAVID "Diagnosis and Remedy in Marx's Doctrine of Alienation," *Social Research,* Vol. XXV (Autumn 1958).

BROCK, WERNER See HEIDEGGER, MARTIN. *Existence and Being.*

BRYCE, JAMES *The American Commonwealth.* London & New York, Macmillan and Co., Second Edition Revised, 1890.

* BUBER, MARTIN *I and Thou.* Second Edition, with a Postscript by the Author added, translated by Ronald Gregor Smith. New York, Charles Scribner's Sons, 1958.

COMMAGER, HENRY STEELE (ed.) *Documents of American History.* New York, F. S. Crofts & Co., 1934.

COMMONS, JOHN R. *Legal Foundations of Capitalism.* New York, The Macmillan Company, 1924.

COSER, LEWIS *The Functions of Social Conflict.* Glencoe, Ill., The Free Press, 1956.

COWLEY, MALCOLM *The Literary Situation.* New York, The Viking Press, 1954.

DAHRENDORF, RALF "Out of Utopia: Toward a Reorientation of Sociological Analysis," *The American Journal of Sociology,* Vol. LXIV (September 1958).

DARVALL, F. O. *Popular Disturbances and Public Order in Regency England.* London, Oxford University Press, 1934.

DAWSON, CHRIS-
TOPHER
"Sociology as a Science," in *Science for a New World,* edited by Sir J. Arthur Thomson and James Gerald Crowther. New York, Harper & Brothers, 1934.

DEEMS, CHARLES T. (ed.)
Christian Thought, Fourth Series. New York, Wilbur B. Ketcham, 1886.

* DESROCHES, HENRI-CHARLES
Signification du Marxisme. Paris, Les Editions Ouvrières, 1949.

DILTHEY, WILHELM
"Der Aufbau der Geschichtlichen Welt in den Geisteswissenschaften," in *Gesammelte Schriften,* Vol. VII. Leipzig und Berlin, Verlag von B. G. Teubner, 1927.

DOBB, MAURICE
Studies in the Development of Capitalism. New York, International Publishers, 1947.

DUNHAM, H. WARREN (ed.)
The City in Mid-Century. Detroit, Wayne State University Press, 1957.

DUNHAM, H. WARREN
"The City: A Problem in Equilibrium and Control," in *The City in Mid-Century.* Detroit, Wayne State University Press, 1957.

FAULKNER, WILLIAM
"On Privacy, The American Dream: What Happened to it?", *Harper's Magazine* (July 1955).

* FESSARD, G.
La Main Tendue? Le Dialogue Catholique-Communiste est-il Possible?, with an appendix "Le communisme, fin de l'aliénation humaine." Paris, Editions Bernard Grasset, 3e Edition, 1937.

FEUERBACH, LUDWIG
"Grundsätze der Philosophie der Zukunft," in *Sämmtliche Werke,* Vol. 2. Leipzig, Otto Wigand, 1846.

FIEDLER, LESLIE A.
"Pull Down Vanity," *Partisan Review,* Vol. XXI (1954).

FINE, SIDNEY
Laissez Faire and the General Welfare-State: A Study of Conflict in American

Thought 1865-1901. Ann Arbor, The University of Michigan Press, 1956.

FORTUNE, *The Exploding Metropolis.* Garden City,
EDITORS OF Doubleday Anchor Books, 1958.

FRANKEL, CHARLES *The Case for Modern Man.* New York, Harper & Brothers, 1955.

FREYER, HANS *Die Bewertung der Wirtschaft im philosophischen Denken des 19. Jahrhunderts.* Leipzig, Verlag von Wilhelm Engelmann, 1921.

FROMM, ERICH "A Counter-Rebuttal" (to Herbert Marcuse), *Dissent* (Winter 1956).

——————— "The Human Implications of Instinctivistic 'Radicalism'," *Dissent* (Autumn 1955).

——————— *Man for Himself: An Inquiry into the Psychology of Ethics.* New York, Rinehart and Company, 1947.

——————— *The Sane Society.* New York, Rinehart & Company, 1955.

* GEHLEN, A. "Ueber die Geburt der Freiheit aus der Entfremdung", *Archiv für Rechts—und Sozialphilosophie,* Vol. XL (1952).

GLAZER, NATHAN "Religion Without Faith," *New Republic,* November 14, 1955.

GUARDINI, ROMANO *Die Macht.* Zürich, Im Verlag der Arche, 1951.

GUARDINI, ROMANO, *Die Künste im Technischen Zeitalter,*
AND OTHERS Dritte Folge des Jahrbuchs "Gestalt und Gedanke," Herausgegeben von der Bayerischen Akademie der Schönen Künste. München, Verlag von R. Oldenbourg, 1954.

GURVITCH, GEORGES *Industrialisation et Technocratie,* Pre-
(ed.) mière Semaine Sociologique (Centre

National de la Recherche Scientifique), Recueil publié sous la direction de Georges Gurvitch. Paris, Librairie Armand Collin, 1949.

HADLEY, ARTHUR TWINING — *Economic Problems of Democracy.* New York, Macmillan Company, 1923.

HALL, STUART — "A Sense of Classlessness," *Universities and Left Review* (Autumn 1958).

* HARRIS, ABRAM L. — "The Marxian Right to the Whole Product" in *Economic Essays in Honor of Wesley Clair Mitchell.* New York, Columbia University Press, 1935.

HEBERLE, RUDOLF — "The Sociology of Georg Simmel: The Forms of Social Interaction," in *An Introduction to the History of Sociology,* edited by Harry Elmer Barnes. Chicago, The University of Chicago Press, 1948.

——————— "The Sociological System of Ferdinand Tönnies: 'Community' and 'Society'," in *An Introduction to the History of Sociology,* edited by Harry Elmer Barnes. Chicago, The University of Chicago Press, 1948.

HEGEL, G. W. F. — *The Philosophy of History,* translated by J. Sibree. Revised Edition, New York, Willey Book Co., 1944.

HEIDEGGER, MARTIN — *Existence and Being,* with an Introduction by Werner Brock. London, Vision Press Ltd., 1949.

——————— *Platons Lehre von der Wahrheit. Mit einem Brief über den "Humanismus."* Bern, Verlag A. Francke AG, 1947.

——————— *Ueber den Humanismus.* Frankfurt A./M., Vittorio Klostermann, 1947.

——————— *Was ist Metaphysik?* Frankfurt A./M., Vittorio Klostermann, 6th Edition 1951.

Translation by R. F. C. Hull and Alan Crick in *Existence and Being*.

———————— "Wozu Dichter?" in *Holzwege*. Frankfurt A./M., Vittorio Klostermann, 1950.

HEINEMANN, F. H. *Existentialism and the Modern Predicament*. London, Adam & Charles Black, 1953.

* HEISS, ROBERT "Hegel und Marx," *Symposion*, I (1948).

HELLER, ERICH *The Disinherited Mind*. Philadelphia, Dufour and Saifer, 1952.

HERBERG, WILL *Protestant—Catholic—Jew—An Essay in American Religious Sociology*. Garden City, N. Y., Doubleday & Company, 1955.

HERTZLER, JOYCE O. *Society in Action: A Study of Basic Social Processes*. New York, The Dryden Press, 1954.

HIELD, WAYNE "The Study of Change in Social Science," *British Journal of Sociology*, Vol. V (1954).

HOBSBAWM, E. J. "The British Standard of Living 1790-1850," *The Economic History Review*, Second Series, Vol. X (August 1957).

———————— "The Machine Breakers," *Past and Present*, Vol. 1 (February 1952).

HOBSON, J. A. *Work and Wealth*. New York, The Macmillan Company, 1926.

HÖFFDING, HARALD *Mindre Arbejder*. Köbenhavn, Det Nordiske Forlag, 1899.

HOMANS, GEORGE C. *English Villagers of the Thirteenth Century*. Cambridge, Harvard University Press, 1941.

* HOOK, SIDNEY *From Hegel to Marx. Studies in the Intellectual Development of Karl Marx*. New York, The Humanities Press, 1950.

HOPKINS, CHARLES HOWARD *The Rise of the Social Gospel in American Protestantism 1865-1915*, Yale Studies

169

in Religious Education XIV. New Haven, Yale University Press, 1940.

HOYT, ELIZABETH ELLIS — *Consumption in our Society.* New York, McGraw-Hill Book Company, Inc., 1938.

HUBERMAN, LEO — *Man's Worldly Goods: The Story of the Wealth of Nations,* New York & London, Harper & Brothers, 1936; Monthly Review Press, 1959.

HUMPHREY, NORMAN D. AND ROSENBERG, BERNARD — See ROSENBERG, BERNARD.

HYMAN, HERBERT H. AND WRIGHT, CHARLES R. — See WRIGHT, CHARLES R.

* JACOBY, E. G. — "Ferdinand Tönnies, Sociologist. A Centennial Tribute." *Kyklos,* International Review for Social Sciences. Vol. VIII (1955).

JANOWITZ, MORRIS — *The Community Press in an Urban Setting.* Glencoe, Ill., The Free Press, 1952.

* KAHLER, ERICH — *The Tower and the Abyss: An Inquiry into the Transformation of the Individual.* New York, George Braziller, Inc., 1957.

KEATS, JOHN — *The Crack in the Picture Window.* Boston, Houghton Mifflin Company, 1957.

KIERKEGAARD, SÖREN — *Kierkegaard's Concluding Unscientific Postscript,* translated by David F. Swenson and Walter Lowrie. Princeton, Princeton University Press, 1941.

* KORSCH, KARL — *Karl Marx.* London, Chapman & Hall Ltd., 1938.

LEDERER, EMIL AND MARSHAK, JAKOB — "Die Klassen auf dem Arbeitsmarkt und ihre Organisationen," in *Grundriss der Sozialökonomik,* div. IX, vol. 2. Tübingen, Verlag von J. C. B. Mohr (Paul Siebeck), 1927.

LEVY, MARION J., JR. *The Structure of Society.* Princeton, Princeton University Press, 1952.

* LEWIS, JOHN *Marxism & the Open Mind.* London, Routledge & Kegan Paul, 1957.

LIPSET, S. M. AND BENDIX, R. "Social Status and Social Structure: A Reexamination of Data and Interpretations," *British Journal of Sociology,* Vol. II (June/September 1951).

LOCKWOOD, DAVID "Some Remarks on 'The Social System'," *British Journal of Sociology,* Vol. VII (1956).

LOHMAN, JOSEPH D. "Political Apathy—Functions of Urban Transition" in *The City in Mid-Century,* edited by H. Warren Dunham. Detroit, Wayne State University Press, 1957.

* LÖWITH, KARL "Man's Self-alienation in the Early Writings of Marx," *Social Research,* Vol. XXI (Summer 1954).

* ———— *Von Hegel zu Nietzsche.* Zürich/Wien, Europa Verlag, Zweite Auflage, 1949.

LUKÁCS, GEORG "Die Deutsche Soziologie vor dem ersten Weltkrieg," *Aufbau* (1946).

* ———— *Geschichte und Klassenbewusstsein.* Berlin, Malik-Verlag, 1923.

* ———— *Der Junge Hegel.* Zürich/Wien, Europa Verlag, 1948.

———— *Karl Marx und Friedrich Engels als Literaturhistoriker.* Berlin, Aufbau-Verlag, 1948.

* ———— "Moses Hess und die Probleme der Idealistischen Dialektik," *Archiv für die Geschichte des Sozialismus und der Arbeiterbewegung,* edited by Carl Grünberg, Vol. 12 (1926).

	Die Zerstörung der Vernunft. Berlin, Aufbau-Verlag, 1954.
* LYND, HELEN MERRELL	*On Shame and the Search for Identity.* New York, Harcourt, Brace and Company, 1958.
LYND, ROBERT S.	*Knowledge for What? The Place of Social Science in American Culture.* Princeton, Princeton University Press, Fourth Printing 1945.
MANNHEIM, KARL	*Ideology and Utopia: An Introduction to the Sociology of Knowledge,* translated from the German by Louis Wirth and Edward Shils. New York, Harcourt, Brace and Company, London, Kegan Paul, Trench, Trubner and Co. Ltd., 1936.
MARCUSE, HERBERT	*Eros and Civilization: A Philosophical Inquiry into Freud.* Boston, The Beacon Press, Second printing 1956.
*	"Die Idee des Fortschritts im Lichte der Psychoanalyse," in *Freud in der Gegenwart,* Frankfurter Beiträge zur Soziologie, Vol. 6. Europäische Verlagsanstalt, Frankfurt am Main, 1957.
*	"Neue Quellen zur Grundlegung des Historischen Materialismus: Interpretation der Neuveröffentlichten Manuskripte von Marx," *Die Gesellschaft, Internationale Revue für Sozialismus und Politik,* Vol. IX (1932).
*	*Reason and Revolution: Hegel and the Rise of Social Theory.* New York, Oxford University Press, 1941.
	"A Reply to Erich Fromm," *Dissent* (Winter 1956).
	"Some Social Implications of Modern

Technology," *Studies in Philosophy and Social Science,* published by the Institute of Social Research, Vol. IX (1941).

* ———————— "Ueber die Philosophischen Grundlagen des Wirtschaftswissenschaftlichen Arbeitsbegriffs," *Archiv für Sozialwissenschaft und Sozialpolitik,* Vol. 69 (1933).

MARSCHAK, JAKOB AND LEDERER, EMIL   See LEDERER, EMIL.

MARSHALL, THOMAS HUMPHREY   *Sociology at the Crossroads,* London School of Economics and Political Science Publications. London, Longmans, Green, 1947.

MARX, KARL   *Capital.* Vol. I, translated by Samuel Moore & Edward Aveling. New York, The Modern Library, n.d.

———————— *Capital.* Vol. I, translated by Eden and Cedar Paul. London, J. M. Dent & Sons, New York, E. P. Dutton, 1957.

———————— *Capital.* Vol. III, translated by Ernest Untermann. Chicago, Charles H. Kerr & Co., 1921.

———————— *A Contribution to the Critique of Political Economy,* translated by N. I. Stone. Chicago, Charles H. Kerr & Co., 1904.

———————— "Debatten über Pressfreiheit," in *Marx-Engels Historisch-Kritische Gesamtausgabe,* div. 1, v. 1, half-vol. 1. Frankfurt A./M., Marx-Engels-Archiv Verlagsgesellschaft M. B. H., 1927.

———————— *Economic-Philosophical Manuscripts,* selected essays from the *Oekonomisch-Philosophische Manuskripte,* translated by Ria Stone. Mimeographed pamphlet,

173

New York, 1947. (A translation of all the manuscripts, announced by the British publishers Lawrence & Wishart, was not yet available at the time this work went to press.)

———————— *Die Frühschriften,* edited by Siegfried Landshut. Stuttgart, Alfred Kröner Verlag, 1953.

———————— "Kritik des Hegelschen Staatsrechts," in *Marx-Engels Historich-Kritische Gesamtausgabe* div. 1, vol. 1, half-vol 1. Frankfurt A./M., Marx-Engels-Archiv Verlagsgesellschaft, M. B. H., 1927.

———————— *Nationalökonomie und Philosophie.* Edited by Erich Thier. Köln und Berlin, Verlag Gustav Kiepenheuer, 1950. See also *Economic-Philosophical Manuscripts* and *Oekonomisch-Philosophische Manuskripte.*

———————— *Oekonomisch-Philosophische Manuskripte,* in *Marx-Engels Historisch-Kritische Gesamtausgabe,* div. 1, v. 3. Berlin, Marx-Engels Verlag, 1932. Also in *Die Frühschriften,* edited by Landshut. (See also *Economic-Philosophical Manuscripts.*)

———————— *Oekonomische Studien,* in *Marx-Engels Gesamtausgabe,* div. 1, v. 3, Berlin, Marx-Engels Verlag, 1932.

———————— "On the Jewish Question," a translation of "Zur Judenfrage," in *Selected Essays by Karl Marx,* translated by H. J. Stenning. London, Leonard Parsons, 1926.

———————— *The Poverty of Philosophy.* New York, International Publishers, n.d.

———————— *Selected Writings in Sociology and Social*

———— *Philosophy,* edited by T. B. Bottomore and Maximilien Rubel. London, Watts & Co., 1956.

———— *Theories of Surplus Value.* Parts of v. 1 and 2, translated by Bonner and Burns. London, Lawrence & Wishart, 1951.

———— "Zur Judenfrage," in *Marx-Engels Historisch-Kritische Gesamtausgabe,* div. 1, v. 1, half-vol. 1. Frankfurt A./M., 1927. p. 576. Also in *Die Frühschriften.*

————AND ENGELS, F. *The Communist Manifesto.* New York, International Publishers, n.d.

———— *The German Ideology.* Parts I & III. Edited with an Introduction by R. Pascal. New York, International Publishers, 1939.

———— *Die Heilige Familie,* in *Marx-Engels Historisch-Kritische Gesamtausgabe,* div. 1, vol. 3. Berlin, Marx-Engels Verlag, 1932.

————AND RUGE, A. "Ein Briefwechsel von 1843," in *Marx-Engels Historisch-Kritische Gesamtausgabe,* div. 1, vol. 1, half-vol. 1. Frankfurt A./M., Marx-Engels-Archiv Verlagsgesellschaft M. B. H., 1927. Also in *Die Frühschriften,* edited by Landshut.

* *Marxismusstudien. Schriften der Studiengemeinschaft der Evangelischen Akademien.* Tübingen, J. C. B. Mohr (Paul Siebeck), 1954.

* *Marxismusstudien,* Zweite Folge, edited by Irving Fetscher. Tübingen, J. C. B. Mohr (Paul Siebeck), 1957.

MC CARTHY, MARY "Dottie Makes an Honest Woman of Herself," *Partisan Review,* Vol. XXI (1954).

MC GINLEY, PHYLLIS — *The Love Letters of Phyllis McGinley.* New York, The Viking Press, 1954.

MEUSEL, ALFRED — *Untersuchungen über das Erkenntnisobjekt bei Marx.* Jena, Gustav Fischer, 1925.

MILLER, ARTHUR — *Death of a Salesman.* New York, The Viking Press, 1949.

MILLS, C. WRIGHT — *White Collar: The American Middle Classes.* New York, Oxford University Press, 1956.

MONNEROT, JULES — *Les Faits Sociaux Ne Sont Pas des Choses,* in Collection Les Essais XIX. Paris, Librairie Gallimard, Cinquième Edition, 1946.

MOORE, BARRINGTON, JR. — "The New Scholasticism and the Study of Politics," in *Political Power and Social Theory.* Cambridge, Harvard University Press, 1958.

———————— "Strategy in Social Science," in *Political Power and Social Theory.* Cambridge, Harvard University Press, 1958.

———————— "Totalitarian Elements in Pre-Industrial Societies," in *Political Power and Social Theory.* Cambridge, Harvard University Press, 1958.

MOORE, STANLEY W. — *The Critique of Capitalist Democracy.* New York, Paine-Whitman, 1957.

NADEL, S. F. — *The Theory of Social Structure.* Glencoe, Ill. The Free Press, 1957.

NATIONAL RESOURCES COMMITTEE — *Technological Trends and National Policy.* Washington, U. S. Government Printing Office, 1937.

ORTEGA Y GASSET, JOSÉ — "History as a System," in *Toward A Philosophy of History.* New York, W. W. Norton & Co., 1941.

OWEN, W. V.   *Labor Problems*. New York, The Ronald Press, 1946.

PARSONS, TALCOTT   *Essays in Sociological Theory*. Glencoe, Ill., The Free Press, 2nd ed., 1954.

────────   *The Social System*. Glencoe, Ill., The Free Press, 1951.

PARSONS, TALCOTT AND SHILS, EDWARD A.   *Toward a General Theory of Action*. Cambridge, Harvard University Press, 1951.

* PLESSNER, HELMUTH (ed.)   *Symphilosophein. Bericht über den Dritten Deutschen Kongress für Philosophie Bremen 1950*. Symposion V. München, Leo Lehnen Verlag, 1952.

POLANYI, KARL   *The Great Transformation*. Boston, Beacon Press, 1957.

REDFIELD, ROBERT   "The Art of Social Science," *The American Journal of Sociology*, Vol. LIV (November 1948).

RENCONTRES INTERNATIONALES DE GENÈVE 1947   *Progrès Technique et Progrès Moral*. Neuchâtel, Les Editions De La Baconnière, 1948.

RIESMAN, DAVID   *The Lonely Crowd. A Study of the Changing American Character*. New Haven, Yale University Press, 1950.

RILKE, RAINER MARIA   *Fifty Selected Poems*. With English Translations by C. F. MacIntyre. Berkeley and Los Angeles, University of California Press, 1947.

────────   *Rilke Poems 1906-1926*, translated by J. B. Leishman. London, The Hogarth Press, 1938.

ROGOW, ARNOLD A.   "The Educational Malaise," *The Nation* (January 26, 1957).

ROSENBERG, BERNARD AND HUMPHREY, NORMAN D.   "The Secondary Nature of the Primary Group," *Social Research*, Vol. XXII (Spring 1955).

ROWLAND, STANLEY, JR. "Suburbia Buys Religion," *The Nation* (July 28, 1956).

* RÜSTOW, ALEXANDER *Ortsbestimmung der Gegenwart: Eine Universalgeschichtliche Kulturkritik.* Dritter Band: Herrschaft oder Freiheit? Erlenbach-Zürich und Stuttgart, Eugen Rentsch Verlag, 1957.

SALOMON, ALBERT "In Memoriam Ferdinand Tönnies (1855-1936)," *Social Research,* Vol. 3 (1936).

SARTRE, JEAN-PAUL *L'Etre et le Néant. Essai d'Ontologie Phénoménologique.* Paris, Librairie Gallimard, 1943.

———————— "The Republic of Silence," in *The Republic of Silence,* compiled and edited by A. J. Liebling. New York, Harcourt, Brace, 1947.

SCHELSKY, HELMUT *Die Skeptische Generation: Eine Soziologie der Deutschen Jugend.* Düsseldorf-Köln, Eugen Diederichs Verlag, 1957.

SCHNITZLER, ARTHUR "Literature," in *Fifty Contemporary One Act Plays,* edited by Frank Shay and Pierre Loving. Cincinnati, Stewart & Kidd Co., 2nd impression, 1921.

SCHULZE-GAEVER-NITZ, G. V. *Social Peace: A Study of the Trade Union Movement in England,* translated by C. M. Wicksteed. London, Swan Sonnenschein & Co., New York, Charles Scribner's Sons, 1893.

SHILS, EDWARD A. "Daydreams and Nightmares: Reflections on the Criticism of Mass Culture," *Sewanee Review,* Vol. LXV (Autumn 1957).

———————— *The Present State of American Sociology.* Glencoe, Ill., Free Press, 1948.

———————— "Primordial, Personal, Sacred and Civil

Ties: Some Particular Observations on the Relationship of Sociological Research and Theory," *The British Journal of Sociology,* Vol. VIII (1957).

SHILS, EDWARD A. AND PARSONS, TALCOTT — See PARSONS, TALCOTT.

SIMMEL, GEORG — *Conflict,* translated by Kurt H. Wolff, and *The Web of Group-Affiliations,* translated by Reinhard Bendix. Glencoe, Ill., The Free Press, 1955.

———— *Der Konflikt der Modernen Kultur.* München und Leipzig, Duncker & Humblot, 2nd ed. 1921.

———— *Philosophische Kultur: Gesammelte Essays.* Leipzig, Werner Klinkhardt, 1911.

———— *Die Religion* (in series *Die Gessellchaft,* edited by Martin Buber). Frankfurt a/Main Literarische Anstalt, Rütten & Loening, 1906.

———— *The Sociology of Georg Simmel,* translated by Kurt H. Wolff. Glencoe, Ill., The Free Press, 1950.

SOMBART, WERNER — *Socialism and the Social Movement,* translated from the sixth German edition by M. Epstein. London, J. M. Dent & Co., 1909.

SPECTORSKY, A. C. — *The Exurbanites.* Philadelphia & New York, J. B. Lippincott Company, 1955.

SPYKMAN, NICHOLAS, J. — *The Social Theory of Georg Simmel.* Chicago, The University of Chicago Press, 1925.

STIRNER, MAX — *Der Einzige und Sein Eigenthum.* Leipzig, Verlag von Otto Wigand, 2nd ed. 1882.

STOUFFER, SAMUEL A.
Communism, Conformity, and Civil Liberties: A Cross-Section of the Nation Speaks its Mind. Garden City, N. Y., Doubleday and Company, Inc., 1955. See also *Look* (March 22, 1955).

——————— "Measurement in Sociology," *American Sociological Review*, Vol. 18 (December 1953).

SUTHERLAND, EDWIN H.
White Collar Crime. New York, The Dryden Press, 1949.

SWANSON, G. E.
"The Approach to a General Theory of Action by Parsons and Shils," *American Sociological Review* (April 1953).

SWEEZY, PAUL M.
"Toynbee's Universal History," in *The Present as History.* New York, Monthly Review Press, 1953. Previously published under the title "Signs of the Times" in The *Nation* (October 19, 1946).

TAYLOR, CHARLES
"Alienation and Community," *Universities and Left Review* (Autumn 1958).

THON, O.
Review of Ferdinand Tönnies' "Gemeinschaft und Gesellschaft," *The American Journal of Sociology,* Vol. II. (1896-1897).

TILLICH, PAUL
Biblical Religion and the Search for Ultimate Reality. Chicago, The University of Chicago Press, 1955.

——————— "Existential Philosophy," *Journal of the History of Ideas,* Vol. V. (January 1944).

——————— *Der Mensch im Christentum und im Marxismus.* Stuttgart & Düsseldorf, Ring Verlag, 1953.

TÖNNIES, FERDINAND
Autobiographical Sketch in *Die Philosophie der Gegenwart in Selbstdarstellungen,* edited by Raymund Schmidt, Vol. III. Leipzig, Verlag von Felix Meiner, 1922.

———————— *Community & Society (Gemeinschaft und Gesellschaft)*, translated by C. P. Loomis. East Lansing, Michigan State University, 1957.

———————— *Fundamental Concepts of Sociology (Gemeinschaft und Gesellschaft)*, translated and supplemented by Charles P. Loomis. American Sociology Series, edited by Kimball Young. New York and Cincinnati, American Book Company, 1940.

———————— *Das Eigentum*. Wien & Leipzig, W. Braumüller, 1926.

———————— *Einführung in die Soziologie*. Stuttgart, Ferdinand Enke, 1931.

———————— "Entwicklung der Soziologie in Deutschland im 19. Jahrhundert," in *Soziologische Studien und Kritiken*. Zweite Sammlung. See below.

———————— *Marx. Leben und Lehre*. Jena, Erich Lichtenstein, 1921.

———————— "Sozialreform ehedem und heute," *Soziale Praxis*, Vol. XXXII (1923) No. 29.

———————— *Soziologische Studien und Kritiken*. Erste Sammlung. Jena, Verlag Gustav Fischer, 1925.

———————— *Soziologische Studien und Kritiken*. Zweite Sammlung. Jena, Verlag Gustav Fischer, 1926.

———————— *Thomas Hobbes: Leben und Lehre*. Stuttgart, Fr. Frommanns Verlag (H. Kurtz), Dritte vermehrte Auflage 1925.

———————— "Zur Einleitung in die Soziologie," in *Soziologische Studien und Kritiken*, Erste Sammlung. See above.

———————— See also Heberle, Rudolf; Jacoby, E. G.; Salomon, Albert; Thon, O.

TOURAINE, ALAIN — "Review of Parsons & Shils," *Cahiers Internationaux de Sociologie,* Vol. XIV (1953).

TOYNBEE, ARNOLD — *Lectures on the Industrial Revolution in England.* London, Rivingtons, 1884.

TRAUB, GOTTFRIED — *Ethik und Kapitalismus.* Heilbronn, E. Salzer, 2nd ed. 1909.

TREATY OF VERSAILLES — *American Journal of International Law.* Supplement Vol. 13, No. 3, July 1919: Official Documents. Oxford University Press, 1919.

TROELTSCH, ERNST — *Augustin, die Christliche Antike und das Mittelalter.* Historische Bibliothek, Band 36. München und Berlin, R. Oldenbourg, 1915.

UNAMUNO, MIGUEL DE — *The Tragic Sense of Life in Men and in Peoples,* translated by J. E. Crawford Flitch. London, Macmillan, 1926.

———————— *Del Sentimiento Trágico de la Vida en los Hombres y en los Pueblos.* Madrid, Renacimiento, 1st ed. 1912.

VEBLEN, THORSTEIN — *The Engineers and the Price System.* New York, The Viking Press, 1934.

———————— *The Instinct of Workmanship & the State of Industrial Arts.* New York, The Macmillan Company, 1914.

———————— *The Vested Interests and the State of the Industrial Arts.* New York, B. W. Huebsch, 1919.

WEBB, SIDNEY AND BEATRICE — *Industrial Democracy.* London, Longmans, Green, Edition 1920.

WEBER, MAX — *From Max Weber: Essays in Sociology,* translated by H. H. Gerth and C. Wright Mills. New York, Oxford University Press, 1946.

———————— *The Protestant Ethic and the Spirit of*

Capitalism, translated by Talcott Parsons. New York, Charles Scribner's Sons, 1950.

WHYTE, WILLIAM H., JR.   *The Organization Man.* New York, Simon and Schuster, 1956.

WOLFE, THOMAS   "The Return of the Prodigal," in *The Hills Beyond.* New York and London, Harper & Brothers, 1941.

WRIGHT, CHARLES R. AND HYMAN, HERBERT H.   "Voluntary Association Memberships of American Adults: Evidence from National Sample Surveys," *American Sociological Review,* Vol. 23 (June 1958).

ZNANIECKI, FLORIAN   "Basic Problems of Contemporary Sociology," *American Sociological Review,* Vol. XIX (October 1954).

ZWEIG, STEFAN   *The World of Yesterday.* New York, The Viking Press, 1943.

Unsigned Articles in Newspapers and Periodicals

Saturday Review, July 28, 1956.
The *Boston Daily Globe,* June 17, 1955.
The *New York Herald Tribune,* August 22, 1954.
The *New York Times,* March 11, 1955; September 7, 1956; December 14, 1956; February 26, 1957; March 2, 1957.

ACKNOWLEDGMENTS

I AM GRATEFUL to Mrs. Franziska Tönnies Heberle, Baton Rouge, Louisiana, for her permission to quote from Ferdinand Tönnies' writings.

Among the friends who have gone over the manuscript and made helpful suggestions I mention especially Elmer Fehlhaber, Ray Ginger, Norman Pollock, and Donald Rasmussen.

I am much obliged to Dr. Barrington Moore, Jr. of Harvard University, to whom I have shown a draft of the book and whose disagreement with some of my ideas has not kept him from examining them with objective understanding. I want also to express my gratitude to Professor Paul Tillich of Harvard University, who once again has proven his friendship by finding time to read the manuscript and to share his thoughts about it with me. Dr. Stanley Moore has edited the manuscript. His concern for detail has been matched by his scholarly understanding of the topic of the book and I am greatly indebted to him for his invaluable help. Whenever I needed advice I could rely on Paul Sweezy who helped me in his generous way. My wife's share in this book is great. Her thoughtful criticism and her technical help have contributed much to my work. While I am indebted to all the persons mentioned I want to exonerate them from any responsibility for the views or for the shortcomings of my essay.

185

It means much to me that my book is published by the Monthly Review Press. The editors and contributors of the *Monthly Review* have often voiced their concern about disturbing developments in our society. They have done so, not because they consider criticism an end in itself, but because they realize that only by understanding and facing the social and moral crisis of to-day can we conquer fear and despair and meet the challenge of working toward a better society. This spirit, I hope, is also reflected in my book.

INDEX OF NAMES

MONTHLY REVIEW

an independent socialist magazine
edited by Paul M. Sweezy and Harry Magdoff

Business Week: ". . . a brand of socialism that is thorough-going and tough-minded, drastic enough to provide the sharp break with the past that many left-wingers in the underdeveloped countries see as essential. At the same time they maintain a sturdy independence of both Moscow and Peking that appeals to neutralists. And their skill in manipulating the abstruse concepts of modern economics impresses would-be intellectuals. . . . Their analysis of the troubles of capitalism is just plausible enough to be disturbing."

Bertrand Russell: "Your journal has been of the greatest interest to me over a period of time. I am not a Marxist by any means as I have sought to show in critiques published in several books, but I recognize the power of much of your own analysis and where I disagree I find your journal valuable and of stimulating importance. I want to thank you for your work and to tell you of my appreciation of it."

The Wellesley Department of Economics: " . . . the leading Marxist intellectual (not Communist) economic journal published anywhere in the world, and is on our subscription list at the College library for good reasons."

Albert Einstein: "Clarity about the aims and problems of socialism is of greatest significance in our age of transition. . . . I consider the founding of this magazine to be an important public service." (In his article, "Why Socialism" in Vol. I, No. 1.)

DOMESTIC: $7 for one year, $12 for two years, $5 for one-year student subscription.

FOREIGN: $8 for one year, $14 for two years, $6 for one-year student subscription. (Subscription rates subject to change.)

116 West 14th Street, New York, New York 10011

Modern Reader Paperbacks